Merry Christmas

Love,
Grandma & Grandpa
Dec 25, 2020

TALES FROM THE
SEATTLE SEAHAWKS
SIDELINE

TALES FROM THE
SEATTLE SEAHAWKS
SIDELINE

A COLLECTION OF THE GREATEST
SEAHAWKS STORIES EVER TOLD

STEVE RAIBLE
WITH MIKE SANDO

SPORTS
PUBLISHING

Photos courtesy of Seattle Seahawks.

Sports Publishing books may be purchased in bulk at special discounts for sales promotion, corporate gifts, fund-raising, or educational purposes. Special editions can also be created to specifications. For details, contact the Special Sales Department, Sports Publishing, 307 West 36th Street, 11th Floor, New York, NY 10018 or sportspubbooks@skyhorsepublishing.com.

Sports Publishing® is a registered trademark of Skyhorse Publishing, Inc.®, a Delaware corporation.

Visit our website at www.sportspubbooks.com

10 9 8 7 6 5 4 3

Library of Congress Cataloging-in-Publication Data is available on file.

Cover design by Tom Lau
Cover photo credit Associated Press

ISBN: 978-1-68358-140-6
Ebook ISBN: 978-1-68358-157-4

Printed in the United States of America

For Sharon.

Thanks for the patience,
the support and the love.

—Steve

CONTENTS

ACKNOWLEDGMENTS

The authors thank the Seahawks for their cooperation. Photographer Corky Trewin came through in the clutch. Gary Wright, Dave Pearson and Michael Lipman were also particularly helpful, as always.

INTRODUCTION

It was the biggest, most delirious celebration Seattle had ever seen. By some estimates, three-quarters of a million people—more than the population of the city itself—jammed downtown streets, sidewalks, and low-hanging tree branches to see their heroes on February 5, 2014. Their Super Bowl Champions.

They ignored the bitter cold and hours-long wait. After all, they had waited 38 years for this day. What was a few more hours? What was a little cold? Through the lean years of losing seasons and even the threat of losing their team, to playoff victories and a Super Bowl appearance under former coach Mike Holmgren, the 12s finally celebrated the world championship they had a very real hand in winning.

Along with my broadcast partners, Hall of Fame quarterback Warren Moon and sideline reporter Jen Mueller, Hawks Hall of Famer Cortez Kennedy, who tragically passed away on May 23, 2017, and one-time team owner John Nordstrom, I rode in a vehicle near the front of the Super Bowl victory parade. The one word we all repeated over and over again during our two-mile trek from Seattle Center to Century Link Field was "unbelievable"! The sea of humanity, the unbridled passion of the fans, the gratitude of the players and coaches—it all showed on a day none of us will forget. It was a perfect end to a remarkable season.

The original version of this *Tales from The Seattle Seahawks Sideline* book went to press in 2004. A year later, the Seahawks were in the Super Bowl for the first time. We updated the book in 2012. The franchise would field its first Super Bowl champion the following season. At this writing, the Seahawks have strung together five consecutive seasons with double-digit victory totals. They had five in their previous 36 seasons combined. So here we are in 2017, eagerly anticipating what might come next for an organization that keeps setting the bar higher still.

Team owner Paul Allen hired coach Pete Carroll and general manager John Schneider in 2010 to rebuild the Seahawks after a couple down years. In four seasons, they delivered the first Super Bowl victory in franchise history. Together, this current Seahawks leadership group has won nine playoff games, two more than the franchise had won in the 34 seasons before their arrival. It's been quite the ascent.

Chuck Knox, Steve Largent and Kenny Easley led the way in making an upstart franchise respectable during the 1980s. Mr. Allen rescued a wayward franchise when he purchased the team and kept it in Seattle a decade later, spearheading the stadium initiative that was a key to it all. Mike Holmgren, Walter Jones, Matt Hasselbeck, Steve Hutchinson and Shaun Alexander helped take the Seahawks to another level in the first decade of the 2000s. The current group reset all expectations just as social media was revolutionizing the landscape. Fans have come to hang on to every tweet from a cast of characters that has included Richard Sherman, Earl Thomas, Kam

Chancellor, Marshawn Lynch, Michael Bennett, Russell Wilson and even the ever-youthful head coach himself.

A fundamentally sound football team underpins it all. This has become a squad built around a couple of pretty simple football concepts: a smothering, fast-twitch defense built from the secondary forward, and a power run game on offense that wears down, then throws over the opposition.

"We lead by example and that's how our team plays," Sherman explained. "Guys follow guys who make plays, and who show up on game days and make big plays in big games. We have all those things, so we have tremendous leadership. They don't have to talk, they don't have to say what they are going to do, they don't have to give a rah-rah speech, but when you need them, they will be there for you."

This team was built predominantly with chip-on-the-shoulder overachievers who love football, hate losing and would do anything to keep from disappointing their teammates. Guys like Chancellor and Sherman, who were practically afterthoughts on draft day as fifth-round selections. Guys like Bennett, who entered the NFL as an undrafted free agent and ultimately turned himself into one of the game's dominant forces on defense. There was also a reclamation project of sorts in Lynch, who was acquired from Buffalo at a discount price and would leave a trail of Skittles along his path to becoming a truly unique icon in the Seattle sports scene.

Oh yeah, these Seahawks also did it with an allegedly too-short, third-round baseball player of a quarterback who became the fastest to fifty wins in league history. From the middle of his rookie season, Russell Wilson has provided the leadership and energy that drives the franchise to this day—and will continue to drive it for years to come. It's easy to forget now that Seattle had put together a pair of 7-9 seasons while Carroll and Schneider restocked the defense during their first two seasons together. The team had invested a substantial sum in Matt Flynn as its potential quarterback of the future when Schneider's hard push to select Wilson changed everything.

For most of their existence, the Seahawks had been on the wrong side of the quarterback ledger. My old teammate Jim Zorn helped make the organization respectable right away. Another of our teammates, Dave Krieg, outperformed all reasonable expectations coming out of tiny Milton College. He helped make Seattle a playoff team in the 1980s, earning three Pro Bowl appearances and joining Zorn in the Seahawks' Ring of Honor. He was underappreciated during his career, but the franchise sure missed his production after he was gone. Solving the quarterback puzzle has always been a difficult task.

Seattle had tried to sign our own Warren Moon as a free agent in 1983, only to have the Houston Oilers beat us out in a bidding war for his services. Eight years later, after Moon was well on his way to a Hall of Fame career, Seahawks coach Chuck Knox was set on drafting another future great in Brett Favre. The team's ownership at the time famously overruled Knox, insisting the Seahawks select Dan McGwire instead. The Seahawks were back near the top of the draft order two years later, but they weren't picking quite early enough. While Drew Bledsoe was the No. 1 overall pick and went to New England, where he would play in a Super Bowl, the Seahawks held the second overall pick and wound up with Rick Mirer instead. The bright future that luminaries as notable as Bill Walsh envisioned for Mirer never materialized.

The franchise's QB fortunes began to turn toward the positive again when Matthew Hasselbeck arrived in 2001 and went on to become a three-time Pro Bowler and Super Bowl starter.

Wilson has taken the torch and run with it like few quarterbacks in league history. Counting playoffs, Wilson led all NFL quarterbacks in rushing yards and ranked 19th in the league overall during his first four seasons, before an ankle injury slowed him in 2016. His ability to escape trouble and create offense is unmatched in all the league. His prowess as a passer has proved many a draft expert wrong. Wilson's 99.6 passer rating over his first five regular seasons ranked fourth in the NFL behind Aaron Rodgers, Peyton Manning and Drew Brees among qualifying quarterbacks over that span. The great Tom Brady was fifth on that list.

Marshawn Lynch may have put Beast Mode and that relentless attitude out to pasture when he left the team following the 2015 season. The offensive line may have gotten too young, too soon as Seattle failed to make a deep playoff run in 2016. The defense may be on its way toward learning what life after the Legion of Boom looks like. But the quarterback with No. 3 on his jersey refuses to "go gentle into that good night." In 2016, Wilson battled knee and ankle injuries that would have sidelined any normal human for weeks. He never threw his impossibly young, inexperienced blockers under the bus, even though they routinely threw him to the wolves (to be fair, their jobs became a lot tougher when injuries derailed every contingency plan at running back, exacerbating the impact felt by Lynch's retirement).

Maybe the greatest thing you can say about a quarterback is that you never feel like you're out of any game with him at the controls. That has certainly been the case for Seattle since Wilson entered the fold. Carroll has preached from the beginning that good things will happen eventually as long as the team continues playing with the relentless fury that has marked his tenure. Wilson has been the perfect quarterback to convert that mantra into reality.

The examples were plenty, even in 2016, when injuries diminished Wilson's magic.

Down 31–18 to Arizona with under three minutes to play in Week 16? No problem. There was Wilson, finding tight end Jimmy Graham and receiver Paul Richardson for a pair of rapid-fire touchdown passes to even the score in the final minute. Seattle trailed by double digits again at San Francisco with playoff seeding on the line one week later. Again, there was no need to panic. Wilson hit tight end Luke Willson and running back Thomas Rawls for touchdown passes on consecutive possessions to give the Seahawks a lead they would not relinquish.

It's been this way since Wilson arrived in 2012. In his first months on the job, Wilson shocked Green Bay and a national Monday Night Football audience with a last-ditch scoring pass to Golden Tate, a connection that Packers fans derisively recall as the Fail Mary. Then, in only his sixth pro start, Wilson shocked the powerhouse Patriots with a 46-yard fourth-quarter bomb to Sidney Rice to secure a comeback victory. The win was special for Carroll because it came against his former employer. It was also when Wilson started cementing belief in his abilities.

"If guys didn't believe in him," All-Pro safety Earl Thomas said after the game, "I guarantee they believe in him now."

The legend has continued to grow. Who could forget the laughably improbable comeback victory over the Packers in the NFC Championship Game after Wilson's third season? The Packers had Wilson's number all day, intercepting four of his passes. But with the season on the line, it was a battered and bruised Wilson lofting a perfectly placed 33-yard touchdown pass to Jermaine Kearse in overtime. "We just kept believing," Wilson would say.

Entering my 42nd year as a part of the Seahawks family, I have been honored to call the biggest plays, the most incredible finishes, and the most heartbreaking defeats in this franchise's history. My friend and partner in this book, Mike Sando, and I hope you enjoy our look at this run of success that rivals any team in the NFL. And that you relish the "old stories" as much as we do of the players and coaches who built this franchise. Finally, we join 12s everywhere in hoping we get to line the streets of Seattle again soon to celebrate your Seahawks—Super Bowl champions.

—Steve Raible, April 2017

It was a simple second-down running play. If you were lucky, you'd get three or four yards. With less than three and a half minutes to play, all the Seahawks wanted to do with running back Marshawn Lynch was "pound the rock" and hang on to an evaporating lead against the defending Super Bowl champion New Orleans Saints.

It was a matchup nobody expected. Seattle arrived at the playoffs as the first division winner in NFL history with a losing record (7-9). And it was a game few outside the Hawks locker room thought first-year coach Pete Carroll's "rebuilding-process" of a team could possibly win. But it was on this raw January 2011 afternoon in Seattle that the Seahawks were reborn. From our broadcast booth at Qwest Field (now CenturyLink Field), Hall of Fame quarterback Warren Moon and I watched the most improbable, impossible play unfold.

"2nd and 10 at the 33. Matthew (Hasselbeck) under center. (Ben) Obomanu goes in motion right to left. Turn and hand to Lynch left side. Finds a little bit of a hole. (LOUDER) Keeps his legs moving. He's across the 40... midfield... he's on the run, Lynch. (LOUDER) 40... pushes a man... 35, look at him go. (YELLING) He's down to the 20, 15... he could go. He is gonna go. (SCREAMING) Touchdown Seahawks!

(CROWD GOES NUTS) Oh my word, a 67-yard run! Marshawn Lynch... unbelievable! He must have knocked five guys down on the way to the end zone. The Beast is alive and well!"

That single play, that remarkable individual and team effort not only shook the football experts down to their shoelaces, it even registered on the Pacific Northwest Seismic Network. Lynch finished with 131 yards, and Hasselbeck threw four touchdowns in Seattle's 41-36 win over the Saints. Entering my 37th year with the franchise as player, analyst and now play-by-play voice of the team, I've seen few plays so dramatic and so consequential.

For after the Holmgren era had passed and Jim Mora's one-year tenure had run its course, Carroll's believers have made believers of us all. The Seahawks enter the 2012 season with the biggest, fastest, most talented Seattle defense since the days of Easley, Jake and Tez. The young offensive line is made up of athletic road graders. And "Beast Mode" is still ... well ... a beast! And for the 12th Man — all those eternally hoarse fans who make Seattle the toughest road game in the NFL — these are the *Tales from the Seattle Seahawks Sideline* with new and updated stories since our first go-around in 2004.

Now as then, special thanks to Mike Sando, to all those teammates and friends who shared their stories, and to the Seahawks for their support and assistance. And to the fans whose cheering for their Hawks will always ring in my ears.

—Steve Raible, August 2012

CHAPTER 1

Chuck

C huck Knox had only two losing seasons in nine years as Seahawks coach. His teams made four playoff appearances during a six-year stretch in the 1980s, and one of those non-playoff teams finished 10-6. That's impressive, particularly since the franchise had never reached the playoffs before his arrival.

Chuck's greatest challenge, his greatest accomplishment, was getting that first team to believe it could win. He brought in some veterans like Reggie McKenzie, Cullen Bryant and Blair Bush. He drafted a difference maker in Curt Warner. But those 1983 Seahawks were largely comprised of Jack Patera's players.

Chuck Knox

Chuck had won with the Rams, of course, and there was a sense about him that the Seahawks hadn't really existed B.C. (Before Chuck). In fact, Chuck issued an order of sorts when he discovered team pictures hanging at Seahawks headquarters: Either write the team records on the pictures, or take the pictures off the walls. Of course, only the 1978 and 1979 teams had winning records. Perhaps that was Chuck's point.

It was as though he were saying, "OK, you guys thought you knew how to play, but you didn't know how to play and here's what you need to know now." That said, he did take them within a game of the Super Bowl that first year, and he did it with 90 percent of Jack's players.

Mike Tice, shown here with a very young Cortez Kennedy, walked into a punishing left hook ... from his own coach.

Chuck by TKO

The bigger they come, the harder they fall. And at six foot eight, Mike Tice was plenty big. He came to us from the University of Maryland in 1981 as a quarterback, if you can believe it. Coaches took one look at big Mike's arm and moved him to tight end.

The switch paid off for all involved. Tice turned into a solid all-around player. He played 14 NFL seasons, including 10 with the Seahawks, and finished with 107 starts, 11 touchdown catches and one knockout loss to Chuck Knox.

That's right, Mike Tice once lost a fight to his head coach. Except it wasn't a fight so much as an ambush.

A skirmish had flared on the field. As Tice fled the sideline to aid his teammates' cause, Chuck intervened with a left hook straight out of the steel mills where he worked summers as a kid.

"Chuck turns, hits me in the gut with a punch, drops me to one knee and knocks the wind out of me," Tice said.

A day later, when players convened to vote on the big hit of the week, their head coach walked off with the award. The whole team went crazy.

"You almost knocked me out," Tice told his coach.

Knox's response was vintage Chuck. "Mike," he said, "if you'd been on my other side and I'd hit you with my right, you would still be down."

Mr. Consistency

Dave Wyman came to the Seahawks as a second-round draft choice in 1987. He played for Chuck Knox and Tom Flores, then left in 1993 to play for Mike Shanahan in Denver. Only then did Dave fully appreciate the coach who brought him into the league.

"I really came to respect Chuck more after I went away and played someplace else," Dave said. "Chuck could be a pretty tough guy, but he was just consistent in the way he approached games, the way he prepared, the way he prepared the team, the way he dealt with players.

"Things weren't personal with Chuck. It was just business. It was just football issues. And Chuck never sold out his players to the media. We loved the fact that he told reporters all those same Knoxisms every day. Then he'd come in and tell us what it was really like. Maybe he would rip us a new one, but he'd do it privately. And he'd tell you to your face what you needed to do to get better, to keep your job, whatever. He didn't throw around compliments readily, but when he did, they really stuck with you."

Air Chuck

People knew him as Ground Chuck, but four of Knox's nine Seattle teams passed more frequently than they ran. His teams were a lot more balanced than one would expect from the nickname he earned coaching the Rams and Bills in the 1970s.

People forget that Chuck's first Rams team featured MVP quarterback John Hadl. Your quarterback doesn't become MVP of the league without throwing the ball. "All I know is if you look at the stats and you see where we ranked, we were running the football, we were throwing it, we were doing whatever was expedient to enable us to win within the framework of the players that we had," Chuck said. "We were the second team in the National Football League to use the shotgun formation. Dallas was first, we were second. We also had a version of the run-and-shoot that we liked to use that was very successful. I don't know how you can call it Ground Chuck. We were not."

Steve Largent only retired as the most prolific pass catcher in NFL history. Daryl Turner averaged nine touch-down catches a season and 18.5 yards a catch from 1984 to 1987. Those teams pounded the ball with Curt Warner and John L. Williams, but they threw it too.

Chuck famously opened a big 1984 game at Denver with an 80-yard touchdown bomb from Dave Krieg to Turner. The Broncos were 11-1 and had won 10 consec-utive games that season. Seattle was 10-2 and had won six straight. Chuck was eager to take the Mile High Stadium crowd out of the game early. Curt Warner was long since out for the season with a knee injury, but Chuck proved he could adjust. So, after consulting with receivers coach Steve Moore during the week, they revealed their big plans to Dave on game day.

There Dave was, walking around thinking about this deep ball all during warmups, all during the national anthem. "Gosh, first play of the game, I'm going up on top, we're going to throw the ball deep. I've got to make this throw." The pass was a little long, but Daryl made an outstanding play and just kept on galloping. There was stunned silence at Mile High. It's never been as quiet.

Dave passed for 406 yards and three touchdowns that day. Largent caught 12 passes for 191 yards. Turner made the big play early. And, most importantly, the Hawks won the game, 27-24.

Toughness Personified

Chuck Knox took a lot of pride in being tough, and also fair. You've got to bring a certain amount of mental and physical toughness to the game, he always said. And his upbringing in Pennsylvania's steel country reflected that.

Chuck's father immigrated from Ireland at age 21. His mother was hired out as a domestic from Scotland at age 20. Chuck and his brother were the first members of the family born in America. They were raised in a tough area and lived in a walk-up flat above a saloon. Suburban America it was not. Chuck's family never had a car or a phone. But, as Chuck pointed out, his father never needed either.

"All he had to do was walk down two blocks and go to the steel mill. His idea of a vacation was not having to go in that steel mill for two weeks in the summer. He would ride around in a beer truck and say hello to everybody. They were going to make deliveries down to the V.F.W. and he'd just ride along and everybody they'd see, he'd stop and B.S. with them at every stop they made."

Chuck worked the three-to-11 shift in the mill in the summers. The old-timers told him to get that education so he wouldn't have to follow in their bootsteps. Chuck never forgot that. He never forgot his roots.

On Top of His Game

We take you to Seattle's one-time jazz mecca for a glimpse into the life of Chuck Knox at the peak of his popularity.

Lofurno's was an Italian restaurant in the New York tradition, situated in a converted three-story home on Elliott Avenue.

Pete Gross and I loved the place. You walked in and the bar was right in front. There was booth seating and, if you preferred, you could sit in the back or upstairs. And you know Chuck: former coach with the Jets, aficionado of a good antipasta, etc. Lofurno's was made for him.

The off season rolled around one year in the late 1980s and Chuck, having heard Pete and I rave about the place, wanted us to take him there. Chuck had grown to like Pete from all the time they spent doing radio. But this was new ground for me; Chuck and I had never really socialized outside of the occasional team-related banquet.

At the coach's suggestion, Sharon and I swung by to pick up Chuck and his wife, Shirley. The four of us met Pete and Bev for a night that showcased Chuck when the Seahawks truly owned the town.

We started out with a glass of wine and we ordered antipasta and then we ordered Caesar salads, then more wine, then maybe a bottle of wine, then dinner came and Chuck was regaling us with these wonderful stories. We were laughing and this little three-piece jazz band started playing in the bar. We could see them from our table.

People were coming over and saying hello to Chuck, and pretty soon there was more wine and after-dinner drinks and, really, we were having a great time.

Somewhere in there I let it slip that I had played drums since age 11, back when my father played in big bands and jazz bands and orchestras. Chuck, in all his glory, walked over to the bar, bought drinks for everyone and headed over to the band. He pulled out $25 and told the drummer to disappear for a while.

"Steve, go up there, sit down and play for a while."

So I went up and played. We were all having fun and carrying on, and now Chuck was telling stories to everybody in the bar. He was surrounded and just really in his element. Shirley and Sharon and Bev were sitting up at the booth, just laughing. This was a normal thing for Shirley: her man was out and amongst his people.

Chuck was just absolutely on target that night, on top of the world, and he loved it. He couldn't have been nicer, or more beloved.

Life at the Day Care

Jack Patera had always allowed players to bring their families to team headquarters on Saturdays. Chuck Knox, unaware of the perk in his first year on the job, grumbled upon entering a locker room filled with kiddies. "What the hell are we running, some kind of day care?"

Chuck Knox said he stayed "true to my colors" by refusing to put on a smile after management drafted Dan McGwire, right, against his wishes.

Everyone enjoyed a laugh when a team official let Chuck in on the arrangement.

We're All Gonna Get Fired

Jim Zorn was retired. Dave Krieg was far from finished, but his days in Seattle were running out. A couple years had passed since the ill-fated trade for Kelly Stouffer, and management wanted to use the 16th pick in the 1991 draft on a quarterback.

The team had needs elsewhere, of course, and Chuck Knox was eager to go in another direction. Draft day rolled around and Knox was in the war room with his staff when owner Ken Behring and president Tom Flores pulled the grizzled old coach out into a hallway. They told Chuck the news he didn't want to hear, that the team planned to use its first pick on the big quarterback from San Diego State, Dan McGwire.

Chuck was not happy. "Well, now, you know, we've got a lot of other needs," he protested. "If you really want to go after a quarterback, there are a lot of other guys out there."

Brett Favre was among them. The future three-time league MVP lasted into the second round. But Knox's pleading went nowhere. Besides, they'd already talked to Dan's agent. McGwire was going to be the pick, period, end of discussion.

And so Chuck came back into the war room and broke the news to his assistants. "Get ready to coach your asses off," he groused, "because we're going to be fired at the end of the season."

And sure enough, they were. McGwire didn't last long, either. Just 13 games spread across five injury-plagued seasons.

"That's the only time in the nine years that I was there that I did not go down the stairs to the pressroom to announce who the first draft choice was," Chuck said. "I had nothing to do with that thing. I was true to my colors. I wasn't going to go down there and make it look like this is something I've given a lot of thought to."

Curt Warner, shown pulling away from the Raiders' Howie Long and Matt Millen (55), was long gone by 1991.

Talent Drain

Most head coaches run their course inside of 10 years. Sometimes their message stops resonating. Other times the game might begin to pass a coach by. Chuck Knox stopped winning in Seattle mostly because he ran low on talent.

Curt Warner, Dave Brown, Steve Largent and Kenny Easley were gone before 1990. Chuck no longer had the personnel he won with in the mid-1980s. It was that simple.

"First and foremost, I think Chuck just had the reins of the team taken out of his hands by (owner) Ken Behring, which is then what happened to Tom Flores," linebacker Dave Wyman said. "It was just really a difficult time in the history of this franchise.

"Nobody really knows how difficult it was until you have a chance to look back and see the squandered draft choices and the awful decision to try to move the football team.

"Everybody kind of tiptoed around it for so long, but he very nearly killed that franchise."

CHAPTER 2

Character and Characters

Not for the Faint of Heart

There have been a lot of tough guys in the NFL. But I've only known one who played with a ruptured testicle. Now that is tough.

Fans today know Paul Moyer as the sideline reporter on our radio broadcasts. But from 1983 to 1989, Paul was a hard-nosed safety who took playing through pain to ridiculous levels. And never more than during a victory over Denver in the final game of the 1986 season.

Paul was the strong safety in coverage when the Broncos sent Orson Mobley on a routine hook-and-go pattern in the first half. Mobley was the Broncos' massive tight end and a good player. He could be a difficult match-up at six foot five and 260 pounds.

Anyway, Mobley ran the route and Paul settled and came up on the hook. Well, when Mobley turned to run the take off, he grabbed Paul's jersey and tried to get past him. And he kneed Paul right in the groin. Paul never wore a protective cup in those days, so he dropped to the ground almost instantly.

The trauma had pushed one of Paul's testicles up into his body, but no one knew the extent of the injury. They iced him down in the locker room at halftime and sent him back onto the field for the third quarter, this time with a protective cup.

There were times in the second half, Paul said later, when the pain nearly made him vomit. But he stayed in the game, knowing a victory would result in a 10-6 record and a shot at the playoffs. The Seahawks won the game, 41-16. And while there would be no playoffs, the disappointment could not match the emotions that sent Paul reeling when he undressed in the locker room.

Paul actually screamed when he looked down and saw the massive internal bleeding that had spread into his back and abdomen. They rushed him into surgery that night.

Fortunately for Paul, doctors were able to save the testicle. Unfortunately for Paul, who was single at the time, the headline in the paper screamed something like, "Moyer plays with ruptured testicle"—not exactly the kind of news a young bachelor wants out there.

Everything worked out in the long run. The toughness Paul showed that day in 1986 probably helped him land coaching jobs with Chuck Knox and Tom Flores.

Drop and Give Me ...
a Piece of Chalk?

Kenny Easley didn't want any help in the weight room, but Joe Vitt wasn't the type of guy to back down. Vitt was the first real strength and conditioning coach we had, and he could be tough. But Easley could be tougher than anyone.

One day when Kenny refused to follow Joe's suggestions in the weight room, Joe kept chipping away at him like a chihuahua, right into the parking lot. After a while of this, Kenny just turned around and cold-cocked him. Dropped him right there in the parking lot. That was Kenny. Push him at your own peril.

"I show up a little bit later," quarterback Sam Adkins recalled, "and somebody had gone out in the parking lot and taken chalk and outlined the body."

The Power to Endure

Joe Nash was the least flashy member of the best defensive line in franchise history. Jacob Green and Jeff Bryant got most of the attention, and deservedly so. But Joe Nash played 218 games for the franchise, most in Seahawks history.

"Joe Nash lasted because he was tough," Chuck Knox said. "What you see is what you'd get. He'd bring his A game every week. He knew the defensive schemes well. He played well with Jacob Green and Jeff Bryant and those guys. He made a lot of big plays.

"He never got the credit because you'd look at him and he's not physically the biggest guy and he's

Joe Nash earned senior-citizen status around team head-quarters.

not physically the fastest guy. But he's smart, he studied film and he played hard."

Mike Holmgren, Fan of the Game

The final regular-season game in the Kingdome served as a bridge between current and former Seahawks. It was December 1999 and Mike Holmgren was still getting acclimated to being a Seahawk, but his appreciation for NFL history was firmly established.

I was down on the field emceeing the postgame activities when Mike leaned over and issued a special request.

"Hey, introduce me to Jack Patera. I've always wanted to meet him."

That was refreshing. Coaches can be so myopic about what they have to do for the here and now. This franchise has meant a lot to a lot of people over the years, and Mike Holmgren seemed to sense it. First and foremost, he's a fan of the game.

Fighting Feasel

Grant Feasel would fight anyone, anytime, anywhere. Thus the nickname, Fighting Feasel. Feasel, who passed away in 2012, was a nice guy in real life. But during his run at center from 1987 to 1993, all bets were off. It just so happened, too, that Grant was a hilarious practical joker.

They would be holding a Saturday morning walk-through practice and Grant would secretly cut out the inseam of his shorts and ditch his jock altogether.

An unsuspecting Dave Krieg would stick his hands under center and, well, at least the offensive linemen thought it was funny.

You gotta love pro football. These guys were nothing but a bunch of overgrown kids when you really think about it.

Pain in the Glass

The old Bellevue Holiday Inn was hardly a five-star resort, but the maids kept some of the cleanest sliding-glass doors in greater Seattle. Ken Meyer, who coached quarterbacks under Chuck Knox, found out the hard way during a meeting one night before a game.

NFL teams generally stay in local hotels on the night before home games to facilitate meetings and minimize distractions.

Ken Meyer and the quarterbacks were making last-minute preparations when Kenny decided to shut the sliding-glass door leading out to the hotel atrium. Except the door was already closed.

He smashed face-first into the window, spilled his drink all over himself and, in a brazen attempt to play it off, immediately turned to the blackboard and began diagramming a play. Didn't miss a beat.

And for the longest time, none of the players said a word. Sure, an assistant coach had just left a detailed imprint of his face on the glass. But this wasn't just any assistant coach. Ken Meyer had played for Woody Hayes and coached under Bear Bryant, to say nothing of his own stint as head coach of the San Francisco 49ers.

If there was a certain amount of respect for a guy like that, well, Dave Krieg would have to pay it another time. Dave started giggling from his seat a couple rows back.

"I don't know if anybody is not going to laugh or not, but that is funnier than hell. He just ran into the door. You're not going to say anything about it?"

Everybody enjoyed a great laugh out of it. Poor Kenny Meyer. The imprint of his face was still on the glass the next day, at least until those maids found their way into the room.

Ron Essink (Call Him Mariah)

Back in the early days, the rookies always had to stand up and sing in the dining hall at training camp. Some guys were just really, truly so desperately awful that nobody would ask them to sing again. That was probably a good thing.

Some of us could sort of carry a tune, so we'd have to sing.

And then others became instant cult heroes, like Ron Essink. He was a national champion wrestler in college who came in with Dave Krieg in 1980, and it was, "OK, rook, get up there, tell us your name, tell us your school, sing a song."

And so he goes, "Ron Essink, offensive tackle from Grand Valley State." And he started to sing "Mariah" by the Kingston Trio. And I mean, I thought he was on stage in a Broadway play. *The rain is Tess, the fire's Joe and they call the wind Mariah*. He was belting it out. *Mariiiiiaaaaah*.

Ron Essink stunned teammates with his singing ability.

Well, he got a "standing O" in the dining hall and his nickname from that day on was Mariah. If he walked in the room right now I'd say, "Mariah! How you doing?" And he'd know exactly what I was talking about.

Every time he got up to sing after that, he sang "Mariah." We wouldn't let him sing anything else because he was so good.

FIRST IMPRESSION:
The Boz

Sizing up linebacker Brian Bosworth was easy for Edwin Bailey. The veteran guard, who for a decade was one of the Hawks' most consistent offensive linemen, took one look at The Boz and knew exactly how to handle the overhyped prospect from Oklahoma.

One of the first times Bosworth assumed his position on defense at a Seahawks practice, Bailey came to the line of scrimmage and planted his paw on the ground, same as he'd done countless times before. Two things stood out as Edwin cocked his head to scan the defense: Bosworth's cartoonishly tiny feet.

Edwin "Pearl" Bailey yuks it up with Brian Bosworth.

They were the smallest feet Bailey had ever seen on an NFL player. The big guard knew instantly that all he had to do was hit The Boz in the middle of the chest, because no player with feet that small could muster enough leverage to tangle with a lineman.

Bosworth relied on his quickness, but with those feet, he had no base.

"All I had to do was square him up and he was mine," Bailey said.

Brian Bosworth Unmasked

Players can sniff out the punks from the teammates who are out there fighting for one another. And despite his obnoxious appearance and antics, Brian Bosworth wasn't a punk. Beneath the goofy hair, the earrings and the cocky shtick was a likeable guy whose puffed-up body simply couldn't take the pounding of NFL life.

Outside the locker room, it was always a me-me-me thing with "The Boz." On the inside, teammates discovered he was a team guy. Dave Wyman credited Brian for helping him get through some nervous moments as a first-year starter in 1988.

"We were good buddies," Wyman said. "He was just as quick as anybody you ever saw play, but it was obvious he probably wouldn't have a very long career just because he wasn't naturally a big, strong guy. You knew that injuries were probably going to get to him at some point."

People forget, too, that Bosworth was actually pretty productive until his shoulder gave out after 24 games. In 12 starts as a rookie in 1987, "The Boz" amassed an admirable stat line: 78 tackles, four sacks, three passes defensed, two forced fumbles and two fumble recoveries.

"Bosworth had a lot of ability," Chuck Knox said. "We didn't get a chance to scout him because we got him in the supplemental draft. We didn't know he was going to be available. It was a 37-to-1 shot. We got him and he could really run.

"He had a big game up in Denver. We had him spying on John Elway because he was the only linebacker we had who was as fast as Elway. He did a good job for us. It was unfortunate that he had a career-ending injury because of the deterioration of the cartilage in his shoulders."

Hard Knocks

Pro football is a tough game played by tough guys. Linebacker Winston Moss played one week after suffering a torn anterior-cruciate ligament in his knee. Center Kevin Glover played a game with a blood clot in his lung. Tight end Mike Tice kept playing after jamming multiple dislocated fingers back into place. Joe Nash played with a broken leg. The stories are endless.

Like a lot of guys, guard Pete Kendall tried to play with concussions, but doctors could always tell when he was bluffing. Kendall would lose his Boston accent whenever he got his bell rung.

Pretty Boy Roche

Receding hairline, freckled face, toothless smile. That was Alden Roche, the defensive lineman who came to us from Green Bay in 1977.

We were at practice on Alden's first day as a Seahawk and the offense broke the huddle. Tom Lynch, who played guard for us from 1977 through 1980, assumed his usual stance. He looked both ways, looked up and there was Alden Roche grinning in all his natural beauty.

Tommy's eyes got real wide and Alden looked at him and said, "Heh, heh. I's ugly, ain't I?"

Comfort Zone

A fter a few years, we started winning some games and getting some confidence. Not that we thought we were great, but now we were starting to become veterans. We were in our fourth and fifth years playing together, and we knew the offense, and we knew what we were doing.

Offensive coordinator Jerry Rhome had coached pretty much the same people since the beginning, with a few exceptions. Zorn, Largent and I were all there from Day One. It was a good feeling.

You still felt the urgency to want to play well and make the team. I certainly did. Obviously Steve and Jim were the stars. But you still felt like when push came to shove that you were gonna make that team. You knew that unless they brought in some guy who was just a fabulous athlete, you had the experience and you knew what Jerry wanted.

And so we started having a little more fun. Jerry liked to spice up training camp with nickname nights. We had nominations and you'd come up with about 10 of them. Then we'd vote and the winning vote would become a guy's nickname. There was no negotiating, either.

Dave Krieg lobbied hard for "Cobra" but nobody cared what they called him at Milton College. We called him Mudbone instead, after the character Richard Pryor made famous in his stand-up routines. Dave hated his new moniker—we can assume Richard Pryor never made it to Milton—but the vets loved it and that's all that mattered.

After all, Dave was just a no-name free agent without a school at that point, Milton College having closed its doors in 1982. No one suspected he would rank among the NFL's top 10 in passing yards when he retired. "When you come from Milton and then the school goes away, you've got to be a pretty humble guy anyway," Dave said.

Zorn was "Z-man" and I was "Peach" because I played college ball in Georgia. Sam McCullum was "Magic" and just so smooth when he ran. Mike Tice was Lurch, for obvious reasons. And Largent became Yoda thanks to the *Star Wars* costume he wore to a Halloween party (his wife actually came as Yoda to Steve's Princess Lea, but giving Steve "Princess" as a nickname wasn't going to work).

To this day I'll call him Steve, but I'll call him Yoda, too, in a heartbeat. That never goes away. In fact, that's the way it was a few years ago when he was in Congress and I visited him at the Cannon House Office Building on Capitol Hill.

I walked in and saw old Yoda across the room. His constituents were in there and his staff and all that, but I didn't care. "Yoda!" And his staff, they were just stricken. This look came over their faces: "How dare you? This is a U.S. Congressman!" And Yoda goes, "Raibs!" And we came over and hugged. That's the way it is. Same thing for all these guys. It just stays with them.

Joe Camel?

Joe Cain smoked like a chimney. Before games, he would lapse into this deep coughing ritual which he claimed would pull air into his backside and push it out through his mouth, purging his body of all toxins. Seriously.

Joe might have been crazy, but he wasn't stupid. The guy actually attended Stanford for a while. He wound up transferring to Oregon Institute of Technology, where he played for future Hawks defensive coordinator Greg McMackin, and somewhere in there guys started calling him Joe Brain. Chad Brown, who played with Cain in 1997, called Joe one of the classic characters he'd ever met.

"Joe was an older guy. He was a backup linebacker, and I guess we got kind of thin on special teams. They put Joe on the kickoff team, and it was his first time running down on kickoff in years. I think he bruised his chest, hyperextended his knee and sprained his ankle all on one play.

"Joe had been through the wars, and at that point in his career he really didn't care what happened. He would cuss at a coach. We were at one of the last minicamps before training camp and we had to do a conditioning test. And Joe looked right at the coach and said, 'If y'all SOBs plan on cutting me, tell me now because I don't want to do this test.' He was only willing to put as much effort as needed at that point in his career."

Mr. Clutch

Norm Johnson goes down as the best kicker in Seahawks history, but for Jack Patera's money, no one could top Efren Herrera. Efren wasn't your typical kicker. He could be cocky and brash, but Jack said he never saw a kicker with more cool in the clutch.

Unfortunately, I was in la-la land courtesy of a Jack Tatum hit when Coach Patera sent Efren onto the field for the kick that gave us a sweep of Oakland in 1978. Jack relayed the story years later.

"Efren was down by my side and I said, 'Now, we're going to roll the clock down to three seconds and I want you to...'"

Efren finished the sentence: "Go out and win it."

That was Efren. And he made the kick, a 46-yarder for the biggest win in franchise history to that point. And eight or nine years after he was retired, Efren still believed he could go out there and win football games. That's just the way he was.

"I would have taken Efren, I think, over any kicker that I was ever associated with," Jack said. "Not because he had the strongest leg or anything, but boy, when it was on the line, he came through."

Weird Al

One time down in Oakland the Raiders were guilty of encroachment before the game even began. Each team was guaranteed access to a given amount of the field during warmups, and the Raiders were sailing punt after punt directly into our allotted area.

So Jack Patera sought out Jim Sweeney, the Raiders' special teams coach at the time, and told him where to go. Sweeney shrugged and told Jack that's the way Raiders owner Al Davis conducted business. Well, Jack was a tough guy and he wasn't going to let that stand.

"To hell you're going to do it today."

Sweeney walked over to Davis, and Jack wasn't far behind. Of course, Al's approach to the opposition was to avoid personal contact at all costs. Al turned and walked away.

That left poor Jim Sweeney, who was between head-coaching stints at Fresno State, to deal with Jack.

Good 'Ol What's-His-Name

Tears welled in Tom Flores's eyes as he took questions following what would become his final game as Seahawks coach. The loss to Cleveland in the final game of 1994 hadn't been pretty.

"I'm tired, I'm worn down, I feel badly," Flores said. "I feel badly for our team and for our organization. This is a high-pressure profession, filled with emotion. You get emotional sometimes, but you try to control it. Nobody twisted my arm to do what I'm doing."

There was nothing funny about it at the time, but that final game featured some laughable personnel arrangements.

Seattle actually went into that season hoping to have the most capable secondary in the league. But nothing went according to plan. A catastrophic knee injury claimed Pro Bowl corner Nate Odomes two months before the season. A bum hamstring knocked out the other corner, Patrick Hunter. A torn Achilles tendon cut down Pro Bowl free safety Eugene Robinson. Injuries likewise also claimed two backup corners.

With the entire starting secondary sidelined, Seattle didn't stand much chance against Vinny Testaverde that day. The situation was so dire, in fact, that freshly signed safety Dion Lambert found himself starting only three days after his first practice with the team.

Another safety, Del Speer, met his new coaches for the first time less than 72 hours before kickoff.

And that was only the half of it.

Weeks earlier, the front office had summoned Terry Taylor, who hadn't played for the team since 1988, back on an emergency basis. Never mind that Terry had already filed his retirement papers with the league. He started the last three games of the season.

The constant shuffling created all kinds of confusion for defensive coordinator Rusty Tillman and secondary coaches Dave Brown and Paul Moyer. Rusty didn't wear a headset in those days, so he would have Dave signal the plays into the huddle. Well, when Rusty tried to unleash a certain blitz against the Browns, Dave had to tell him the bad news.

"We can't do that because the guys we have in there don't know how. They've never practiced it."

Paul tried to tell Dave that a certain player had in fact practiced that blitz, but there was one problem: Paul couldn't remember the player's name. His exact words to Dave were to put "what's-his-name" in the game so they could run that blitz. And Dave just started to laugh, right there on the sidelines, during the game.

Taylor was actually making the incomplete-pass sign below his knees, his way of telling Rusty to choose a play they had actually practiced.

It was a credit to those guys that the 1994 defense actually entered that Cleveland game ranked 12th against the pass. But the season was a lost cause, and ownership fired Tom Flores five days later.

Chasing Warren Moon

Semantics prevented Warren Moon from becoming a Seahawk in 1984. That's the way Chuck Knox sees things, anyway. Knox met with Moon and agent

Leigh Steinberg in Miami, but the former University of Washington passer didn't sign with Seattle until 13 years later. By then, Warren had played eight Pro Bowls.

"I thought we had a good shot at him," Knox said, "but the problem came down to this: Our management with the Seahawks did not want to give any guaranteed contracts. You get into semantics here, because if you give someone a signing bonus and it's a big one, that's the same thing as giving them a guaranteed contract. The money is gone and you're going to look a lot longer at that particular player because you have the financial commitment.

"Our people couldn't see it that way and got stuck on semantics and what constitutes a guaranteed contract. That was the sole hang up."

The Seahawks already had Dave Krieg, of course. Warren suspected that was the reason Seattle's management wasn't willing to go over the top with its contract offer. Houston made the better offer and Moon became an Oiler, just like that.

Second Time's a Charm

When the Seahawks finally landed Warren Moon in 1997, he rewarded them by leading the NFL's top-ranked pass offense that year. Warren passed for 409 yards and five touchdowns during a 45-34 thumping of the Raiders in the Kingdome.

Odd as it seems, Warren wasn't even the starter when that season began. John Friesz was more familiar with Dennis Erickson's offense. Here was this guy in Warren who had thrown for like eight miles, and he was backing up a journeyman. Friesz suffered a broken thumb in the opener, however, and Moon was suddenly the man.

Warren liked what Dennis was doing offensively, and he liked the personnel on hand. Joey Galloway, Chris Warren, Michael Sinclair, Chad Brown, Cortez Kennedy, Sam Adams and Shawn Springs had talent.

Friesz got all the snaps in camp, though, and that made life difficult for Warren. He was rusty during an 0-2 start in which the Jets and Broncos outscored Seattle by a 76-17 margin. But Dennis rallied the troops. He told Moon to get ready to throw the ball, and that's exactly what the Seahawks did.

Zorn to Moon and Back

Few people know this, but our first offensive coordinator played a role in the development of not only Jim Zorn but also Warren Moon. Jerry Rhome was coaching quarterbacks in Minnesota when Warren came to the Vikings after his long run in Houston.

"I learned more about what a real NFL quarterback is supposed to do in a pro-style offense from Jerry Rhome," Warren said. Those Houston teams ran the run-and-shoot all those years, so Warren hadn't played in a traditional NFL offense until he met up with Jerry in the 1990s. And of course Warren parlayed that experience into a record-setting season with the Seahawks in 1997.

And so it was that Jerry Rhome's first Seattle quarterback made a name for himself by being unconventional, by rolling out, throwing on the move, burning defenses with the sprint-draw, etc. And Jerry got a great deal of credit for that. Years later, Warren gives Jerry a lot of credit for showing him how to be a more classic NFL passer.

Tight Ends, Good Friends

There's something with Warren Moon and tight ends. He remains close to former Chiefs teammate and Pro Bowl tight end Tony Gonzalez. Deems May is another close pal, strange as it seems.

Two more different guys, you couldn't find. Here's this North Carolina country guy, Deems May, with his drawl and a big wad of tobacco jammed into his lower lip. And then here's this suave quarterback out of Los Angeles who has played in a number of different cities around the National Football League.

And yet these two guys hit it off and have a close friendship. Deems was one of those guys you had to have on your team. He gave everything he had and other players picked up on the example.

This Little Piggy
Went to the Redskins

Peter Cronan was a one-of-a-kind prankster whose exploits often crossed the line, even by locker-room standards. We called him Piggy when he played linebacker for us in the late 1970s. You'll soon discover why.

Finding suitable Piggy stories is a challenge. But here goes.

In our old locker room, they used to keep the towels near the toilets. Where some saw linens and plumbing, Piggy saw opportunity. Let's just say that unsuspecting rookies would leave the showers, fumble for a towel and ... nah, can't tell that one.

But here's one more. Piggy won a Super Bowl with the Redskins after we cut him loose. A mutual friend of ours, Mark Cherry, went to visit him at the Redskins' hotel before the big game. They met in the lobby and, of course, it was packed.

Piggy wasn't paying much attention. He backed up a little bit and then backed up a little more, right up against this pillar. He looked around and kept talking to Mark, but by now the back of his pants were within earshot of this poor woman who was seated next to the pillar. So they're talking and ... well, guess that one won't make the book, either.

This one will: Piggy used to come in from practice all sweaty and grimy, then strip naked and bounce from one Nautilus machine to another. "OK," he'd say between sets, "your turn."

No thanks, Piggy. We'll sit this one out.

Nothing's Sure

Don Bitterlich was a third-round pick from Temple in 1976. He earned a roster spot and started preparing for a long run as placekicker. Except they cut him after three games, and poor Don was just beside himself. I don't blame him. It was difficult.

You don't know anything for sure until all those cuts are finally made. And even then, as Andy MacDonald always said, "Don't buy wall-to-wall carpeting. And if you do, don't nail it down because you just don't know where you're going to be and what's going to happen next."

Best Athlete He Saw

With apologies to his 15-touchdown season in 1990, Derrick Fenner didn't exactly establish himself as one of the premier players in franchise history. His career with the Seahawks lasted only three seasons and 23 starts. But Derrick Fenner was certainly among the best athletes to come through the Emerald City. Linebacker Dave Wyman, whose Seahawks career ran from 1987 to 1992, called Fenner the best pure athlete he played with in Seattle.

Derrick was the most incredible athlete Dave ever saw on a basketball court, in the locker room, in the weight room, all those things. He was cut, he was big and there wasn't an ounce of fat on him. He could jump out of the gym and he was fast for a guy his size. He had great moves, great quickness and, despite some off-the-field problems, Derrick also had a wonderful personality.

Did he achieve all he could have achieved with the God-given ability he had? Probably not. Did he get as much as possible out of that specimen-like body? Probably not. But he was a stud.

Dan Fouts

Spend a few years in the NFL and you'll play against some of the all-time greats. Dan Fouts was one of the best we ever saw during the Seahawks' early years. Dan was one of those bad-body guys who never won any beauty contests, but what an incredible "game" player he was.

In 1977, Dan held out for the Chargers' first 10 games. During that time, he returned home to Oregon and basically just watched his beard grow. When he finally came back, there were the Seahawks on the schedule for a November 27 date in the Kingdome.

Dan hadn't even practiced, but he threw for about 12 miles on us (actually 279 yards on 19-of-24 passing, with two touchdowns).

San Diego won the game, 24-20, and we had to tip our caps to Dan Fouts. The guy was at home playing pitch and catch with his kids for three months and he still went out and destroyed us on short notice. That's the kind of player Dan Fouts was, and why he was an easy pick for the Pro Football Hall of Fame.

Rick's Rep

Ricky Watters could be a train wreck waiting to happen, but what a competitor. All he wanted to do was win. Let me re-phrase that. All he wanted to do was have a chance to help the team win. And if he wasn't getting that chance, he let people know about it. That's where Ricky's reputation came from. It wasn't because he was selfish, as so many outsiders thought. It was because he wanted to win so badly and he knew he could help the team.

The thing about Ricky, too, was that he never made mental mistakes. Well, almost never. He went the wrong way on a 1998 play in Kansas City and the result, unfortunately, was that Warren Moon suffered broken ribs and the season began to slip away.

FIRST IMPRESSION:
Curt Warner

Watching Curt Warner run 60 yards on his very first regular-season carry illustrated right away why some of these guys are picked among the first handful of players in a given draft. They are just so far superior as athletes to the other guys out there. Curt Warner was special that way, and you could see it from Day One.

Curt Warner, Out for the Year

The air went out of the Kingdome when a knee injury cut down Curt Warner in the 1984 opener against the Browns. Curt came around the right side on a little pitch play. He planted and then hopped as his right leg went limp.

That split second altered the season as well as Curt's career. The Seahawks won that game, 33-0, and the team won more games (12) than any in franchise history. But losing Curt for the season changed that team.

Those Seahawks beat the Raiders in a first-round playoff game, but they couldn't get past the Dolphins in the second round. Steve Largent's six-catch, 128-yard day down in the Orange Bowl meant little as the running game managed only 51 yards in a 31-10 loss. Dan Marino was on a mission, too, and the Dolphins rode his arm to Super Bowl XIX.

Curt Warner came back from the injury and had some very good seasons, but the knee wasn't the same. He was never able to make the kind of speed cuts and fluid

Curt Warner breaks into the clear during Seattle's 1983 AFC playoff game at the Orange Bowl in Miami.

cuts that defined his rookie season. It was too bad. Then again, Curt was always more than just a football player. Intelligent and hard working, today Curt has a beautiful family and a low handicap. And he's still one of my favorite Seahawks.

Diaper Change

Robbie Tobeck was sicker than a dog. Make that sicker than a horse. The Seahawks' affable center developed some sort of infection, possibly from the horses his family raises, and the ailment was threatening to keep him out of the lineup.

This was seven weeks into the 2001 season, and the Seahawks, at 3-3, needed a victory at Washington to creep above .500. Robbie didn't practice that week, but he gutted it out come Sunday. Unfortunately for quarterback Matt Hasselbeck, Robbie suffered a major-league accident as he fired out of his stance on the first offensive series.

One of the very next plays called for the shotgun formation, but crowd noise at FedEx Field forced Hasselbeck to cozy up under center. Matt knew something was wrong, but he couldn't quite put his nose on it. He gained a more complete understanding when one of the trainers offered some advice.

"Hey, I'd stop licking my hands if I were you."

The trainer came over a little later with a slick, clear disinfectant. Rubbed it all over Matt's hands. Before long, Matt was losing a fumble and tossing two interceptions—all in the first half. One pass slipped from Darrell Jackson's grasp, right to a defender.

Coach Mike Holmgren lost his temper at halftime, Matt lost his job for the second half and Seattle lost the game, 27-14.

Thankfully, the equipment guys didn't lose their sense of humor. Upon returning to FedEx Field in 2003, they rigged Tobeck's locker with Depends Undergarments on the Saturday before the game. Robbie wore them, too, leading to a hilarious scene as Holmgren passed through.

Exactly what a head coach needs to see: one of his team captains parading around the locker room in an adult diaper.

Cracks in the Ceiling

Football players aren't the brightest guys, Jack Patera used to say. And too often the evidence backed him up.

One Saturday morning in the Kingdome, Jack turned to Don Testerman, a fullback who played for us from 1976 to 1978, and pointed to an imaginary crack in the ceiling.

"Looks like that one big crack is getting bigger."

Testerman looked around. "What crack?"

"You know, that one crack that is standing out. It's getting bigger and bigger."

Confusion was turning to concern. "My God, what should we do?" Testerman asked.

"Well, I think it will hold until practice is over."

Testerman started pacing around, looking at the ceiling, worried that the sky would be falling at any time.

The NFL Life Cycle

Bob Newton played 11 years in the NFL, first with the Bears and then with the Seahawks. Drugs and alcohol might have prevented him from playing 15, and Fig knew it. When the end finally came, on the final cuts before the 1982 season, Jack Patera summoned the old veteran for the meeting every player dreads.

"Bob, you've been one of our guys for a while now and I'd love to say that we want to keep you on. But we've got to make some decisions. You know how it goes. We'll bring you back if somebody gets hurt, so we want you to stay in shape."

What Jack said next stuck with Bob.

"Normally, Bob, in this situation we'd probably keep an extra offensive lineman. But we've decided to keep an extra defensive lineman this year. That's a little unusual, but we decided to do it because we think this one kid has a little bit of promise and we just want to see what we can do."

The kid with a little bit of promise was free-agent nose tackle Joe Nash, whose career spanned 15 years and a team-record 218 games.

Fig wasn't bitter. He tried out for the USFL, but never made it. Then, on July 12, 1983, the day his old Seattle teammates reported to training camp, Bob Newton admitted himself to drug and alcohol rehab. He's been sober ever since.

To beat it the way Bob has, and to do what he has done, is just a great tribute to him.

Surreal Homecoming

Mike Holmgren couldn't walk five feet without running into an old friend, or perhaps a camera crew attempting to capture the moment. His first game back at Lambeau Field was played, quite appropriately, under the lights of *Monday Night Football.*

Unsure how the Packer faithful might greet a coach who was now the enemy, Mike had discouraged his own daughters from attending that 1999 homecoming game. And yet the remarkable warmth and appreciation shown by the Packer faithful was mostly lost on Green Bay's former coach, at least until afterward. There must have been 100 cameras and press guys around Mike as he tried to navigate the field area before Seattle's blowout victory. He couldn't see much of anything. But the fans truly appreciated what he'd accomplished.

Mike Holmgren hoists the game ball after Cortez Kennedy and Ricky Watters carried the Hawks past Green Bay in Holmgren's first game back at Lambeau Field.

After all, Mike had done what Packer legends Bart Starr and Forrest Gregg couldn't do. He had done for their fans what hadn't been done since the days of Vince Lombardi. He had brought an NFL championship to a town that had forgotten how to win.

P.J. Goes to Copenhagen

With nicknames like "Country" and "Mudbone" it's no wonder John Sawyer and Dave Krieg dipped snuff in prolific quantities. As for the wiry receiver we called P.J., well, Paul Johns should have known better. This was back in the early '80s, before all the Surgeon Generals' warnings.

Watching Country and Mudbone indulge themselves was enough to prod P.J. into giving the stuff a try.

Now, a number of us every so often would have a cigar or something like that, and still do. But you ask a guy like Dave Krieg, who dipped for 20-some years, and he'll tell you that's a tough habit to break.

But Paul was determined. "Yeah, I'm from Texas ... we have that stuff down there."

So Paul takes this big old pinch and sticks it down there in his lip and within minutes he was as green as grass and just gagging. He was spitting 20 times every 10 seconds, but inevitably some of the juices made their way into his stomach. He was so sick and he pretty much learned at that moment that never, ever again would he do anything like that.

When he wasn't gagging on Copenhagen, Paul Johns was a dangerous return man from 1981 to 1984.

He got a lot of grief because of that, too, shoving a big old wad in his lip and just gagging himself silly.

Veteran Leadership

We had veteran leadership from our linebackers that first year. Mike Curtis won a Super Bowl with the Colts. Ed Bradley had gotten some playing time in Pittsburgh when injuries kept Jack Lambert off the field. Ken Geddes was just a great guy and a good player, too.

You'd always know "Geddo" was in the building because of his laugh. And to this day if Ken Geddes laughs, I laugh and everybody around him laughs. It's just infectious. He's such a warm guy with such a great personality. He played a couple seasons with us. Had a broken arm for a while and played through that.

Some of those characters were just such great fun, such great guys to learn from.

Mike Curtis and the Hanky Bowl

The first game the Seahawks ever won featured 35 penalties and zero style points. The Hanky Bowl, they called it. And we won it, I'm convinced, because the crusty old linebacker we landed in the expansion draft was just sick and tired of being out there so long.

Mike Curtis blocked a field-goal try with 42 seconds left and we got out of there with a 13-10 decision.

In the hot Tampa Bay sun, it just seemed like an eternity out there, which was one reason Mike was so disgusted and he was just going to end it right here. To this day, only one game in NFL history suffered from more penalties (Cleveland and Chicago combined for 37 in 1951). Overtime was not an option as far as Mike was concerned.

Now, I knew Mike Curtis was an awfully good player in his day. He had been one of the big stars in the league defensively. The guy won a Super Bowl with Baltimore. But sometimes you don't truly appreciate a veteran teammate until your own career gets some seasoning.

My rookie year was Mike's 12th year. He had been a high-round draft choice out of Duke. He was an academic All-American as a fullback and a linebacker, and as everyone said, he was tough as nails, truly one of the toughest football players around at the time. He played both inside and outside linebacker and was pretty beat up by the time he got here, but knew how to play the game. And he knew how to intimidate.

We learned about that early in camp that first year, 1976. First thing in the morning, we'd get to the training room to get taped up and Curtis would walk in and, I swear to God, he had a face that would stop an eight-day clock. Just gnarled and lined and looked ... just scary. Eddie McMillan, the old corner we picked up from the Rams, gave Mike the nickname "Face."

A veteran could do that. But to all of us rookies, we just tried to stay out of Mike's way. He was the only player coach Jack Patera ever had who handed over a gun when Jack outlined the rules against bringing firearms to camp. It was an old horse pistol. That was Mike Curtis. We'd see him out after practice and he'd be doing his own drills that he had done for years. You looked at his body and it didn't look like he ever lifted a weight. He had no real definition to speak of, but he was just tough. And for some reason, he kind of took a liking to me. He called me "Kid."

And we'd trade stories. He was very intelligent and a good conversationalist, just a little different. But I figured if this guy's been in the league 12 years, he must know what he's doing. So I watched him. And at the pregame meal, instead of downing steak and eggs like the rest of us, Curtis never touched anything on his plate.

All he did was drink coffee, like eight or nine cups. He would leave early for the stadium to get extra taping, and he'd drink more coffee there. And he'd just sit around the locker room and read the press guide with his feet up. That's the way he prepared for a game.

Well, for about three weeks, I did the same thing. Curtis would go out there and play an entire game and play like a madman, and all I did was keep running to the bathroom. I couldn't even make it through pregame warmups. And I had the shakes.

Sometimes you learn from the veterans what not to do as much as what to do.

Steve Niehaus, Non-Bust

We weren't world beaters our first season, but No. 1 draft choice Steve Niehaus certainly met expectations with 8.5 sacks. Steve was the NFC's defensive rookie of the year and even better off the field.

The Seahawks wanted Niehaus all the way, but to the folks outside the draft room, running back Chuck Muncie was another option. Niehaus had knee problems at Notre Dame, but he was big and fast and a two-time All-American with just a great first step. He came from a solid background, too. Then you had Muncie, who had experienced nothing but problems and was considered a bad-attitude guy and all that.

When it came time to pick, with a defensive-minded coach in Jack Patera, the Seahawks took Niehaus with no reservations. Steve led the team in sacks as a rookie. He was as quick as anybody I ever saw on the defensive line. He looked to me like a guy we could anchor a defense around for 10 years.

But a shoulder injury changed everything. Steve just wasn't the same. And he never said much about it. Today, most guys would be out of the lineup in a heartbeat. Their agent would be on the phone. In those days, you didn't have anybody like that looking out for you.

To this day, people say the Seahawks screwed up from the very first draft by picking Steve Niehaus. But that was not a bad choice. That was a great choice. It was an unfortunate way things happened for him in his career, but he was a good football player and a good guy.

One Cool Cat

Perhaps no coach in Seahawks history was respected more than Tom Catlin. "Tomcat" earned All-America honors playing for Bud Wilkinson at Oklahoma in the early 1950s. He won an NFL championship as a linebacker/center on the 1954 Cleveland Browns. In Seattle, as defensive coordinator during the Knox years, Tom Catlin won the reverence of players and opponents alike.

And his defenses won games.

"He may have been the best coordinator I ever coached against," said Larry Kennan, the longtime former Raiders assistant who later worked with Catlin in Seattle under Tom Flores. "When I was at the Raiders for all those years, we were both real good and had all those epic battles, and Tom was fabulous."

Catlin was a brilliant tactician with a knack for calling the right play at the right time. He knew how to judge the confidence of his players, and how to use that in shaping his play calling. But he might have been even better as a teacher of the game.

"Tom used to go up to the blackboard and he'd get ready to diagram a defense and he'd tell us to hold our questions 'til he was finished," former linebacker Dave Wyman said. "He was so meticulous and so patient and so smart about how he explained it that there were never any questions at the end. That was pretty incredible from a coach."

Middle linebackers are constantly looking to the sideline so they can relay the next play into the huddle. They also glean subtler feedback. When Wyman turned to the sideline and saw Catlin with his poker face and even keel, there was great confidence that Tom always would have them in the right position.

Wyman was a Stanford-educated guy who would dissect your financial portfolio after games. He was also this big, thick thumper who would stone-cold hit you. One time in 1989, after a fight with Pro Bowl Giants center Bart Oates, Wyman returned to the sideline in a rage. There was Catlin to greet him, calm as ever.

"David, do you know where you are right now? Do you know what's going on?"

Wyman's screaming and cursing told the coach all he needed to know. Catlin simply turned and walked away. That's the kind of coach Tom Catlin was: always in control, and all business.

Man of Few Words

When Tom Catlin was an assistant with Buffalo under Chuck Knox, the Bills' coaching staff enjoyed a rewarding home victory over a Rams team they had built into a winner. Don Klosterman and Jack Faulkner were among the friends Chuck and Tom left behind in Los Angeles, and Catlin spotted them on the visitors' bus outside Rich Stadium.

Catlin was never one to say much, but when he spoke, his words carried weight. Seeing Klosterman and Faulkner in the bus, he knocked on the window and motioned for them to step off. Neither knew what to say.

Catlin looked at them and decided to break the silence himself. "The word, gentlemen, is congratulations."

The Other Two Times

Tom Catlin wouldn't take dinner breaks during extended film sessions. Instead, he would load up maybe a dozen celery sticks with peanut butter, then munch on his creations quite obliviously, very nearly driving defensive backs coach Ralph Hawkins over the edge.

But that defensive staff worked well together, and Catlin was unmistakably the leader. One time, when special assignments coach Joe Vitt left the team to undergo cancer treatments, Catlin allowed Randy Mueller to help with defensive preparations.

Randy, then a personnel assistant in his 20s, felt obliged to come up with something significant.

"I'd have something that I thought was huge, some great tendency. Eight out of 10 times they do this, or 10 out of 15 times they do that. And he looked at me one day and he said, 'Well, that's no good. What about the other two times?' And he'd just look and walk away like I was the dumbest guy in the world. That's why he was the coach. Tom Catlin was a beauty."

Keith Butler, Unsung Hero

Michael Jackson made the big plays. He was the great talent with more than enough speed, energy and enthusiasm to dominate from his outside linebacker position. But just as Dave Brown and Kenny Easley anchored the secondary during the Seahawks' most successful seasons back in the 1980s, Keith Butler was the linebacker who held together the front seven.

Keith came from Memphis State to Seattle when Jack Patera was still coaching the Seahawks. He really began to flourish when Tom Catlin arrived as defensive coordinator under Chuck Knox. Tom ran a 3-4 scheme with Butts and either Shelton Robinson or Fredd Young as the inside backers. Bruce Scholtz and either Jackson or all-time tough guy Greg Gaines played the outside.

That was an outstanding linebacking corps and Keith Butler was the guy who held it all together inside. A guy like Fredd Young tended to freelance, and when he did, Butler was there to make sure it didn't get them into trouble. Keith was really an extension of Tom Catlin on the field: quiet, effective and always on task.

Off the field, Keith was just this country boy with a silver tooth in the front of his mouth from when he got his teeth jacked up sometime years ago. He was a tough guy, too. With Butler on the field, it was going to be a fight all day long.

Guys like Michael Jackson got a lot of credit, and deservedly so. But Butler was one of the unsung guys who made that defense work.

Family Feud

An NFL team can be like one big, dysfunctional family. Tennessee's Steve McNair lost the ball during a 1998 game in the Kingdome, but it was Seattle's Sam Adams who lost his cool. It all began when Titans running back Eddie George beat Seahawks defensive end Matt LaBounty to the ball for a fumble recovery. The recovery sustained a long drive, forcing Seattle's defense to stay on the field.

"Damn, LaBounty, we tired, man," safety Jay Bellamy griped.

Big Sam rushed to defend his fellow lineman's honor. "Sam smacks Jay's helmet off his head like 20 yards," cornerback Shawn Springs said. "I run over there to calm Sam down, but he thinks I'm running toward him to help Jay. And he grabs my facemask and starts giving me gut shots.

"And you know how big Sam is. I'm like a rag doll getting body blows from this dude right in the middle of the field. Then Darryl Williams comes over and jumps on Sam, starts hitting him in the ear. Then Jay comes back with his helmet and it's like three DBs jumping this big lineman in the middle of the field on the same play.

"It was the dumbest thing I've ever seen."

Seattle still managed to win the game, 20-18.

Making a Splash

Rusty Tillman, our old special teams coach, has to be right up there with the all-time characters.

I can picture him running down the sideline when the opposing team was returning a punt for a touchdown. One time, he ran full speed and literally body-blocked an entire orange bucket full of Gatorade onto the sideline. He'd go berserk sprinting and knocking stuff around and screaming and yelling. It was just comical.

Test Time

Jerry Rhome taught us that the NFL was much more a mental game than perhaps we'd ever known football to be. He was our offensive coordinator and he was constantly testing us. We would take written tests on airplanes or the Friday before a game or whenever.

And for a few years in there, sometimes we had only three receivers who really played a lot. So we had to know all of those spots for each other's positions because we played them all. There was a lot to know.

Dave Krieg used to tell the story about Jerry giving these tests to us. We'd all get 99s and 100s and his looked like somebody bled all over it because it was all red marks by the time Jerry got done with it. That was just part of the deal and so, mentally, we always did great on the test. I was a great test taker.

There were days when I didn't exactly do the job on the field, but I sure got good grades on the tests. That's what I learned from Jerry, how to prepare mentally.

Three Guys Who Fared OK

Mike Holmgren's Seahawks boasted a talented trio of receivers who call themselves "The Three Amigos"... Darrell Jackson, Koren Robinson, and Bobby Engram. They're playmakers on the field, best buddies off it.

The Hawks' original three-receiver set produced a four-term U.S. Congressman, a highly successful businessman and a local news anchor. Not too bad considering our decidedly humble NFL roots.

Steve Largent arrived from the Houston Oilers in August 1976. The price: an eighth-round draft choice. Sam McCullum, originally a ninth-round choice of Minnesota in 1974, landed in Seattle as a Vikings castoff in the expansion draft. I was the last of three second-round choices for the Seahawks in that inaugural draft.

Sam McCullum ran smoother routes than just about anyone.

Raible, Largent and McCullum are still smiling after all these years.

All Largent did was play 14 years, go to the Hall of Fame and get elected to Congress four times. He went on to lead a corporation that lobbied for the wireless industry.

Sam was a fine player for the six years that he was in Seattle, consistent and steady, one of the smoothest route-runners I ever saw. He and his wife, Kathy, have sent two sons, Jamian and Justin, to Stanford on athletic scholarships.

McCullum is now retired and enjoys golf and travel with Kathy.

I'm the runt of the bunch... once described as "a much better anchor than wide receiver." Still, I haven't done all that badly for myself. Six years in the NFL and now 32 years in the same city at the same station, including 28 broadcasting

Seahawks games and more than a decade anchoring the news at KIRO-TV.

We were all kind of kids when we came here to Seattle, so we all grew up here, and then Sam and I stayed and got married and he had a family and we put our roots down.

A lot of players who came here from other cities ended up staying here because of the area. It's so nice, it's a great place to raise a family and the people here were just so darn great to us. The community was just so good to us, and it made it an easy decision for me to stay after six years.

All-Time Seahawks Team

Some of these are easier than others. Steve Largent and Brian Blades at receiver. Walter Jones at left tackle. Mike Tice at tight end.

Jacob Green, Joe Nash and Cortez Kennedy on the defensive line. Dave Brown at cornerback. Kenny Easley at strong safety. Norm Johnson as the kicker.

Things get a little trickier from there.

My guards are Edwin Bailey and Steve Hutchinson. Hutch is already one of the all-time best players on this team as far as offensive linemen. Pete Kendall is one of those guys I also considered at guard, but he didn't play here all that long.

Kenny Easley was an easy choice at strong safety. He would have been even better at free safety, and early on Kenny probably could have played cornerback as well.

Cortez Kennedy collects one of his three sacks during a 1999 victory at Lambeau Field. Tez was an easy choice for the all-time team.

OFFENSE (14)
WR #1: *Steve Largent*
WR #2: *Brian Blades*
WR #3: *Doug Baldwin*
TE #1: *Mike Tice*
TE #2: *Jimmy Graham*
OT: *Walter Jones*
OT: *Russell Okung*
G: *Steve Hutchinson*
G: *Edwin Bailey*
C: *Robbie Tobeck*
QB: *Russell Wilson*
RB: *Curt Warner*
RB: *Marshawn Lynch*
FB: *John L. Williams*

DEFENSE (12)
DE: *Michael Sinclair*
DE: *Jacob Green*
DT: *Cortez Kennedy*
DT: *Joe Nash*
LB: *Chad Brown*
LB: *K.J. Wright*
LB: *Lofa Tatupu*
LB: *Bobby Wagner*
CB: *Dave Brown*
CB: *Richard Sherman*
SS: *Kenny Easley*
FS: *Earl Thomas*

SPECIAL TEAMS
PK: *Norm Johnson*
P: *Jon Ryan*

HEAD COACH
Pete Carroll

An Assist from Trevin

Only a preseason game? Hardly. Trent Dilfer's triumphant return in the summer of 2003 meant so much more. The emotions of that night washed over Seahawks Stadium in waves.

"I was just trying not to cry, and I failed," Matt Hasselbeck said. "He's meant a lot to me as a person, and I'm just really happy for him that tonight was a success."

Four months earlier, five-year-old Trevin Dilfer lost a courageous battle with a heart infection. All thoughts were with the Dilfer family—Trent in particular—when the Seahawks' beloved quarterback ran onto the field during that August 23 game against Kansas City. Fans cheered loudly while teammates hoped for the best.

"It was sort of like I get when I watch my little brothers play," Hasselbeck said. "I was anxious. I really just wanted him to do well, and I really can't say enough about what he has meant to this team and what he has meant to me as a person, as a friend and all that."

With an assist from Trevin, Trent completed his first four passes and 12 of 14 overall, a stunning performance under the circumstances. With his wife Cassandra and three young daughters seated among the faithful, Dilfer played better than anyone had reason to expect.

"It was just awesome," Hasselbeck said. "And to look up at where his family was sitting and to see them going crazy and celebrating ..."

Dilfer's 19-yard touchdown pass to Koren Robinson made the night complete. Robinson dove for the ball, determined to reward Dilfer with a memorable moment. He later delivered the game ball to Dilfer.

"The only thing I can really say is that through this situation, all eyes have kind of been on him," Hasselbeck said. "And from his friends to his coaches to people that don't really know him well, I think that 100 percent of us would say that we admire him more that we ever thought we could. That's all I can really say."

All the Way Back

Trent Dilfer began the day by accepting the Steve Largent Award. He finished it by throwing the clinching touchdown pass to Bobby Engram, shortly after injuries knocked Matt Hasselbeck from the game. As Seahawks Stadium erupted in celebration, Trent leaned over to Bobby with a fitting message: "That one was for Trevin."

Anyone there that day could sense the emotion. And while the December victory over Arizona was critical in the 2003 Seahawks' drive to the playoffs, the way it happened meant more to Dilfer than anyone could know.

"I'm so thankful that Matt convinced me to come play football. It's been really one of the richest years of our family's lives.... These guys have done more for me than I've ever done for them."

The Largent Award is given annually to the player who best exemplifies the spirit, dedication and integrity of the franchise.

"It allows me to feel like I am having an impact on my teammates' lives, that they have somehow been impacted positively by me being around. I take a great deal of pride in that. Every day I go to work with that in mind, to make the people around me better."

In Memory of Trevin

The strength of the Dilfer family continues to inspire. Trevin Scott Dilfer will always live in their hearts, through the TD4HIM Foundation and, most poignantly, through the letter they crafted for the funeral ...

Dear Trent & Cassandra,

On November 10, 1997, I am going to bless your lives with a son. He is my child, but I want you to care for him as if he were your own. Even now, I am weaving him in you, his "Mama". You will love his blonde hair, blue eyes and long lashes that will be coveted by his aunts. He will be a wonderful son, brother, grandson, nephew and friend. Many will appreciate his sensitivity and protectiveness toward his sisters, and he will be famous for his competitiveness; especially when his uncles are involved. You are really going to enjoy this kid.

I want you to teach him about me and prepare him to spend eternity with me. I love him more than you will ever be able to comprehend. He will have a complete life, and he will change your lives forever. In a little more than five years, I am going to bring him home. Although this will be difficult for you, I promise you will understand in due time. You can trust me on this, for I too let a son go.

I have chosen your family for this special child. His life will draw hundreds to me. I have prepared you for this. I will give you the strength to be great parents for him.

I love you more than you could possibly know,
Your Heavenly Father

Trent Dilfer hoists the Steve Largent Award, awarded to him by a vote of his teammates.

Dave Brown,
Consummate Pro

Dave Brown is the kind of player you build franchises around. He wasn't the flashiest and didn't get all the headlines, but Dave was the type who taught younger players how to be great football players and how to be great teammates. We were lucky to have him.

Pittsburgh made Dave its first-round pick in 1975. But the Steelers were so loaded with talent that they left Dave exposed in the expansion draft a year later. He started at free safety his first year with us, but Dave made his mark after moving to cornerback in 1977.

Dave worked harder than anyone I can recall. He was always in better shape, always studied more film, always did whatever it took to separate himself. Dave could be cocky, and you have to be to play that position well. But he could also back it up. Over the years, no matter how many different players they brought in on the other side, there was always Dave Brown playing cornerback for the Seahawks.

Not many teams are blessed with a Dave Brown in the secondary from Day One. We were, and that's one reason we finished above .500 in our third and fourth seasons.

Through Eugene Robinson and others, Dave's legacy impacted the next generation of defensive backs in Seattle.

Dave went on to become cornerbacks coach under Tom Flores and Dennis Erickson, and he was a wonderful coach. He had played the game at its highest level. So, while other coaches told Shawn Springs how to play the game, Dave could actually get through to him.

Hunting Time

Chuck Knox had a simple philosophy in how to utilize the many talents of the Big Dog.

"I loved him," Chuck said of Cortez Kennedy. "We were going to play a four-down lineman scheme and he was going to line up there at right defensive tackle in that left-handed stance where he played at the University of Miami.

"I told George Dyer, our defensive line coach, 'Just put him down there and let him go hunt! Let him hunt!' And that's what he did. He was outstanding. Cortez, he meant a lot because he was quick, he could run and he could clog up that middle and rush the quarterback."

Dave Brown introduces himself to the Dolphins' Nat Moore.

Chuck Knox knew what he had in Cortez Kennedy.

CHAPTER 3

Crazy Days

Some of the stories seem too far-fetched to be true. But trust us, you couldn't make this stuff up. We didn't always win a ton of games in those early years, but we had a helluva good time trying.

Halftime at the 7-11

Bob Newton is director of business development at the Betty Ford Center in California. He's also a chemical dependency counselor who spent 10 years as a substance-abuse consultant to the Seahawks.

Bob Newton talks with line coach Howard Mudd.

But when "Papa Fig" came to the organization in 1976 he was an alcoholic and cocaine addict who happened to be a pretty talented offensive lineman as well.

In the huddle on Sundays, if we could see the whites of Bob Newton's eyes, we knew it would be a long day, because Bob didn't play his best unless he was hung over. Lucky for us and unlucky for Bob, he tended to be hung over more times than not. He'd be the first to tell you that.

Back in the day, Bob drove a customized blue van with "Halftime" emblazoned on each side. One morning in the off season, Bob called me around 10 o'clock with a mini-crisis of sorts.

"Hey, Raibs, can you drive me over to pick up my van?"

"Well, sure. Where did you park it?"

"It's over at the 7-11. I pulled in last night, I'd had too much to drink and I never even got out of the van.

I had turned off the motor to get out of the van and the next thing I know, there was a police officer tapping on the glass to wake me up."

Bob had fallen asleep right at the steering wheel. They didn't arrest him because he wasn't actually driving at the time. But they weren't going to let him drive home, either. So they locked up the van and drove Bob home. Bob was grateful.

The next morning, we set out to find Halftime.

"All right," I said, "so it's at the 7-11? This one right up here?"

"Well, I think so."

"What do you mean, you think so?"

"Well, I'm not sure which 7-11."

We went to six of them before we found Halftime in all its glory. Bob felt terrible, but he had a problem. To drive away and then forget where your car is, that was a pretty sure sign. He's come a long way in the years since.

John Matuszak, Offensive Coordinator

We were pounding the Raiders in the Kingdome back in 1978 when the coaches decided to give Jim Zorn a deserved rest. Steve "Stony" Myer came in at quarterback for the final minutes. And even though we led, 27-7, offensive coordinator Jerry Rhome wanted to give Stony a chance to throw some passes. No one wants to go in late and hand the ball off every time, and Jerry sympathized.

So Jerry started calling passes. And pretty soon, John Matuszak started going nuts. "The Tooz" was six foot eight, close to 300 pounds and certifiably deranged. He would threaten to take your head off, then do it. And his message to Stony was clear.

"What the @!#$% you doing throwing the ball in the fourth quarter? Lookit, you guys are kicking our ass. You throw another pass and ..."

"Hey, I'm not calling the plays. They're coming in from the sidelines."

The Tooz was unimpressed. "You throw another pass, I'll BREAK YOUR @!#$% LEG."

Sure enough, we threw another pass.

"I told you, I'll break your @!#$% leg."

And Steve goes, "I'll audible."

No Passing on the Right

Driver safety became a hot topic in the early 1980s after two high-profile NFL players, Gabe Rivera and Steve Little, suffered paralyzing auto accidents while departing their respective training camps.

Coach Jack Patera had already driven the point home in 1977, informing the team that the Washington State Patrol knew camp was about to break. But not everyone listened. Greg Collins, a linebacker we picked up from San Francisco in 1976, drove a yellow Porsche 911. And like everyone else, he couldn't wait to get out of Cheney once camp broke. You would check in for lunch, you'd eat and then you'd get on the road back to Seattle.

Well, Greg and Jim Zorn were the last ones out of Cheney that year. So the rest of us were driving down the road on Interstate 90 and all of a sudden we see this yellow blur. Whoooooooosh! And Greg Collins's Porsche just blows by everyone at about 130 mph.

He was driving around people on the right shoulder, doing all this other crazy stuff, and did I mention he had the quarterback in the car with him?

And so they get to Issaquah, not far from Seattle, and they come around this bend and the 911 slides off the road right into this hill. Rain had just started falling and the 911, with the engine in the back, couldn't hold its ground. Wham! No one was hurt, luckily, but word of the mishap filtered back to Coach Patera.

The next day, Jack comes out to practice and pulls Jim aside during warmups. "Jimmy, were you involved in an auto accident yesterday?"

"Yeah, but it was..."

"Thank you. Greg Collins, can I see you?"

That was Greg's last day with the team. Jack cut him. And while Jack claims to this day that the auto accident was not a factor in the release of Greg Collins, it sure couldn't have helped.

When in Rhome (or Cheney), Wear a Rug

Jerry Rhome was a good offensive coordinator. But like a lot of football coaches, his fashion sense wasn't always there. This wasn't the NBA with Pat Riley and the $3,000 suits. Picture, instead, paunchy men in those hideous nylon coaching shorts. In Jerry's case, the affliction extended all the way to the cranium.

Training camp would begin with Jerry asking us to come by his dorm room to pick up the playbook. I remember banging on Jerry's door at 7 o'clock one night, just as he had asked, only to get no response. So I banged again, this time real hard.

I eventually put my ear to the door, and it was clear someone was in there. I could hear a radio and the shower going. Well, about five seconds later, the door opened ever so slightly and it was Jerry. He was peering out like a little old lady who was home alone.

"Hey, you said to come get the playbook."

"Yeah, all right."

So Jerry closed the door and retreated into the room. When he opened the door again, he was dripping wet, wearing only a towel and a baseball cap, which seemed curious.

"Do you always take a shower with a hat on?"

Jerry didn't say a word. He just kind of looked at me.

"Here, here's your book."

Out at practice, we were running plays and Thom Fermstad, our video director, was dutifully recording every moment from high atop his tower. Anyway, Jerry was poring over his list of plays when Jim Zorn came rolling out toward the sideline. Before Jerry had time to react, Jim was right up on him. And he hit Jerry with this glancing elbow, much like a left cross.

And in one white flash you saw Jerry's rug stand straight up like a raccoon. And Jerry's first move was, "SAVE THE HAIR!" His arm went up and he pressed the toupee back down onto his skull in a fraction of a second. Entertaining stuff.

As we went back into the locker room, Jacob Green turned to Sherman Smith and cracked up. "Smitty, Smitty! You see your boy Jerry? How 'bout that rug!" What Jacob didn't know was that Jerry was standing right behind Smitty. That explained why Sherman didn't react in kind.

Meanwhile, Fermstad put together a custom video cut that kept zooming in closer and closer before freezing with Jerry's rug standing straight up. All you saw was this white flash on the film.

A few years later, when Jerry and the staff were let go, Jerry took off his hairpiece in the training room, set it on one of the tables, walked out and never wore it again. That was one move nobody could second-guess.

Dave Kraayeveld, the Original 12th Man

The Broncos beat us in overtime one season with an assist from our 12th man. The year was 1978 and Dave Kraayeveld, a defensive lineman who played with Dave Krieg at Milton College, had recently joined our roster off waivers from the Cowboys. We won't soon forget his initial contribution.

Denver's Jim Turner missed a 23-yarder from the left hash, only to get a second chance because we had 12 men on the field. Turner made the 18-yarder after officials erroneously spotted the ball in the center of the field. In any event, Kraayeveld was the extra man. And he was crying in the locker room after the game.

In Dallas, it turns out, the personnel for field-goal defense consisted of the players already on the field for the previous down. Kraayeveld didn't know any better. He stayed on the field and we paid a heavy price.

Yet, while Kraayeveld's mistake cost us the game, he didn't lose his sense of humor. Years later, after the Seahawks honored fans with a 12th Man dedication, Kraayeveld turned to Krieg at a golf tournament and said something to the effect of, "I'm kinda proud to be a Seahawk now that they named the 12th Man after me."

Nick Bebout, Comedian

Jack Patera unveiled a special speech before a Monday night win over Atlanta, with comical results. This was our first Monday night game and Jack was concerned about our comportment.

"We don't need people looking into the camera and saying, 'Hi, mom,' because everybody has a mother. And I don't want to see any of this 'we're No. 1' stuff because we sure as hell aren't No. 1."

You get the idea. So we recovered the onside kick to wrap up the win and Nick Bebout, one of our offensive linemen and a hilarious guy, decided to pull Jack's chain right there on the sideline.

"Jack! Jack! Is it all right if we say, 'We're No. 4?'"

Boogie Days

Chuck Knox put an abrupt end to rookie hazing after someone rushed into a rookie's room and unloaded with a fire extinguisher. The rookie complained, and Chuck absolutely unloaded on Jacob Green, who was one of the veteran ringleaders.

No one was immune before Chuck arrived. In 1982, when Jeff "Boogie" Bryant was a rookie at camp, the veterans confiscated his clothes from the training room following the afternoon practice. Jeff walked across campus to his dorm, in broad daylight, wearing only his underwear.

The veterans laughed and laughed. Jeff seemed OK with it, too, not that he had much choice.

A fully clothed Jeff "Boogie" Bryant accepts the game ball from hazing opponent Chuck Knox.

Junebug Patera

Jack stopped practice one day for no apparent reason. Puzzled players and staff could only laugh at what came next.

"One of the ballboys had found a junebug out on the field, one of those big ones that flew pretty good," Randy Mueller said. "Jack stopped practice, gathered us all around and tied a string onto this junebug. It was like a harness around the junebug. Everybody watched in amazement at this big bug that Jack was flying around.

"Jack was awesome."

Don't Hit the Guvna

Jack Patera once made an exception to his previously ironclad no-refreshments policy. A visit from then-governor Dixie Lee Ray prompted Jack to stop practice and break out the popsicles for everyone, including the guv herself.

They were banana popsicles and they made our mouths as dry as popcorn. It was just awful. It might have been those days when we had six straight days over 100 degrees.

Dixie Lee was standing on the sideline when a play came directly toward her. Robert "Heartburn" Hardy, the stout defensive tackle with the squeaky lit-

Jack Patera towers over Gov. Dixie Lee Ray. That's personnel man Mike Kellar with hands on hips.

tle voice, could be heard above the crowd. "Don't you hit the guv-na, don't you hit the guv-na."

And it stopped everyone in their tracks. They were all laughing. Heartburn always had something funny to say about something.

Thom Fermstad, the One and Only

The NFL's culture of accountability extends beyond players and coaches. Thom Fermstad has attended every game in franchise history, including preseason and playoffs, as the team's one and only video director. He's the guy responsible for filming each practice and game, then making sure the videos are edited and available to coaches.

Attending more than 40 seasons of games isn't easy. Two late nights nearly cost Thom back in his hard-partying days.

October 16, 1977: Fermstad stumbles home at 5 a.m. and accidentally sleeps until 12:30 p.m., a half-hour before kickoff. "I was out the door in 30 seconds, but I never thought about game-day traffic." Fermstad somehow made it to the Kingdome with only seconds to spare. A co-worker had set up his camera high above the field. Fermstad peered through the viewfinder just in time for kickoff.

September 27, 1980: Fermstad again stumbles home at 5 a.m. He awakes at 10 a.m. this time, but the team plane had already left for Washington, D.C. Panicked, Thom packs up the team's video gear and boards a commercial flight out of pocket. With Jack Patera set to begin film-study sessions at 9 p.m., Fermstad rolls into the team hotel at 8:55.

The Seahawks win the game, 14-0, and general manager John Thompson greets Thom with a welcomed message on the flight home. "Don't worry about reimbursing us," Thompson said.

Fermstad wasn't so fortunate after a late night at training camp in Cheney one year. He flipped a co-worker's new car at 2 a.m. The crash sent Fermie hurtling through the glass t-tops. Thom was lucky to avoid serious injury, but he slipped in and out of consciousness over the next couple hours. A friend drove him from the hospital back to training camp at around 6:30 that morning.

The way Jack Patera saw things, that meant Thom was back in time to film the morning practice from his portable tower. And so Thom did, albeit with a chaperone to make sure he didn't pass out and fall the roughly three stories.

Everyone was accountable, dammit, even a video director with shards of glass still embedded his head.

Out of His Jock

Robert "Heartburn" Hardy was one of the guys responsible for launching Dave Krieg's career. He and Manu Tuiasosopo were the guys who sandwiched poor Steve Meyer, inflicting a career-ending back injury that cleared the way for Krieg to make the team.

Heartburn was like a fire hydrant. You could hit him with a truck or a grinder or an axe and you wouldn't hurt him. He had this squeaky little voice and a good sense of humor. The joke was on him the day he showed up for practice with his jock on the outside of his shorts. Nobody noticed until Heartburn got down in a three-point stance and his jersey rode up a little bit. It was as though he'd gotten confused or was half-asleep when he dressed that morning.

The people in the stands really didn't notice right away, but the guys on the field did. Jack Patera didn't laugh all that much during practice, but he did that day.

Rousseau, Anyone?

Sam McCullum had this drill where he would tiptoe along the 50-yard line as if to work on his balance. For Jack Patera, the sight brought to mind images of Narcissus tiptoeing up to the pond for a better look at his reflection. And finally Jack couldn't help himself.

"Sam, you ever hear the story about Narcissus?"

"Huh?"

McCullum was at football practice, not a symposium on 18th century French comedies. But Jack pressed on.

"I'm afraid you're going to end up just like Narcissus."

"How's that?"

"Well, Narcissus was a guy that loved himself so much and couldn't get enough of himself. He would look at his image in the pond until one time he fell in and drowned."

Jack thought he was being clever, but the analogy sailed right over Sam's head. But that was Jack: a lot more worldly than a lot of people would have guessed.

Think Before You Run

We were down in Miami to play the Dolphins in 1979 and Mark Bell was running with this herky-jerky motion during the Saturday walkthrough. Mark wasn't sure whether Jack wanted the drill run at half or full speed. His funky gait betrayed his indecision.

"Mark Bell, what the hell were you doing?"

"Uh, coach, I thought..."

"Well, that's the problem! Every time you think, you hurt this team!"

Coaches can be cruel. Mark, who played tight end and defensive end for us, surely got the message.

Happy Halloween

Steve Largent came as Princess Leia. His wife Terry was Yoda. I was Slim Whitman. Sharon, my wife, cut a rubber ball in half, jammed the domes under a tight sweater and, God bless her, came as Dolly Parton.

But no one could touch Theotis Brown as Aunt Jemima. To this day I laugh until tears come to my eyes just picturing Theotis at that Halloween Party. Now, could you do that today? I don't know. But at the time, because we were all so close and because Theotis thought it was funny too, we all just about died.

Fraternal Order of Stumpy Legs

Steve Largent, Peter Cronan, Joe Nash and Jim Jodat were among those who qualified for the Fraternal Order of Stumpy Legs. In the early days, any Seahawk whose inseam measured 30 inches or less was a F.O.S.L. They actually had T-shirts.

Teeing Off with Easley

Each morning during training camp, Kenny Easley and Sam Adkins would sign in at the breakfast table at 5:30, drive the 15 miles to Spokane's Indian Canyon Golf Course, play 18 holes and be back at camp by 7:45. They had the course to themselves and sometimes had to double back to various holes they skipped to avoid sprinklers.

Where's Eddie?

Ed Marinaro's better days were behind him when Jack Patera brought him to the Seahawks from Minnesota for a couple games in 1977. Eddie never was the fastest guy, anyway, but Jack was appalled when he showed up and clocked a laughable 5.3 seconds in the 40-yard dash.

"We paid for like three or four weeks for him to train to get in shape so he could get below five seconds," Jack recalled years later. "I mean, he was just in terrible shape."

When Eddie finally signed and showed up and started practicing with us, we all ended up at the Velvet Turtle, an Eastside restaurant we frequented after practice. Eddie came along one day and he turned to Bob Lurtsema, who he knew from the Vikings, and Eddie asked the group who he needed to hang out with, who thought like him, that sort of thing.

And Lurtsy looked right at me. So from that moment on, Marinaro and I became fast friends. That was a tough year for me, because I probably did a little too much partying. Ed, by the way, went on to acting with a very successful career in movies and TV, including *Hill Street Blues*.

Eddie only played in two games for us, and the conclusion to this story might help explain why.

We were freezing our tails off in Kansas City one time when Andy MacDonald, our running backs coach, decided to get Eddie into the game. It was a third-down play, but Andy couldn't find his man.

"Marinaro, Marinaro! Eddie, Eddie!"

Eddie was sitting over on the bench with his cape pulled up to hide his face. The last thing he wanted was to go into the game. They ran the next play without him and then Eddie appeared almost on cue.

"Yeah, coach, what?"

"Damn, kid. I'm sorry. I was going to try to get you in the game."

A Little Something for the Effort

That extra $20 or $30 from Coach Patera could make your Monday. Jack would pull out a wad of bills to reward individual efforts on special teams, and by our reactions you would have thought he was giving out another month's paycheck.

While most of us never made $100,000 in a season, we made decent money. No matter. Whoever got that extra special-teams cash ended up buying beer at Hector's bar that night.

It was a unifying thing where everybody would laugh and carry on when Jack identified the hit of the game and so forth. Even if it was a forgettable game, and we had a fair number of those in the early years, that was one of the things that made special teams really fun.

The NFL frowned on such practices, of course, but Jack didn't care. When he was a rookie in Baltimore, coaches would give them $25 or a new hat for big plays (everybody wore hats in those days).

"I never played for any other team that did that, but I thought it was fun to make it interesting," Jack said.

Art Kuehn, Meet Bob Newton

Bob Newton was eager to make a positive impression with his new coach. Leveling teammate Art Kuehn on a punt return didn't help. Artie was on the coverage team when Fig unloaded on him out of instinct, momentarily forgetting he no longer played for the Bears.

Fig had never played on special teams. He blocked for the Heisman Trophy winner, Johnny Rodgers at Nebraska, after all, so this stuff was new to him. Well, Artie was going down on coverage and Fig took this perfect arc and just drilled him right in the earhole.

Jack Patera proceeded to inform Fig that his uniform was now blue. Fig was so used to wearing black, and he was probably under the influence of something, anyway.

R-E-S-P-E-C-T

One of our rookies in 1977 had a pretty good voice. But when he went to belt out Aretha Franklin's "R-E-S-P-E-C-T" as part of his dining-hall obligations, well, let's just say that Mike Jones probably didn't win his high school spelling bee.

He couldn't spell the word. But he tried anyway.

"R-E-S-P-C-E-T ... you know what it means to me!"

FIRST IMPRESSION:
Mike Holmgren

A three-story banner greeted Mike Holmgren as he stepped onto the field at training camp for the first time as a Seahawk. Jack Patera, Chuck Knox, Tom Flores and Dennis Erickson had made similar walks before him, but something was different this time. Holmgren was only recently removed from the Super Bowl championship he'd brought to Green Bay, for one. The sprawling banner, replete with Holmgren's own triumphant visage, conveyed a sense of fanfare that was unprecedented in franchise history. Holmgren remembers the moment well.

"I had two thoughts. The first was, 'Man, am I a lucky guy. I have come such a long way from coaching football and teaching mechanical drawing at Sacred Heart High School in San Francisco.' I knew I was blessed and I was doing what I wanted to do. I was really just so much looking forward to this opportunity with this organization."

The second thought hit him at almost exactly the same time. "Don't screw this thing up. I don't want to let people down. I don't want to mess it up for a lot of other people."

The Agony of Victory

In 1979, we won our first Monday night game by a 31-28 count at Atlanta. Steve Bartkowski took the Falcons down the field for a late touchdown, but we recovered the onside kick to save the victory.

And so everybody was thrilled. Game balls for everybody. And we look over and here's Brian Peets, one of our tight ends, and he's crying his eyes out. Sam Adkins went over to investigate.

"What's the matter? Are you all right?"

Brian clearly wasn't all right. "I don't know where I live!"

The poor guy got dinged in the head on the onside kick and nobody knew it.

The Adkins Mustache Diet

Fans today know Tom Jackson from his time as the affable analyst on ESPN's *NFL Primetime*. There was nothing affable about Tom Jackson the NFL linebacker. Just ask my good friend Sam Adkins. Sam's last stand as our No. 2 quarterback came after Jackson's Denver Broncos knocked Jim Zorn out of the 1980 season finale.

A little history: A couple weeks earlier, Sam had actually run over an unsuspecting Jackson. Our offensive coordinator, Jerry Rhome, told Sam in no uncertain terms that he'd never see the field again if he tried to run over another linebacker. We were short on quarterbacks as it was, so Jerry didn't want to lose another one.

Well, Sam goes into the rematch and right away, he has to make a choice. It was a play-action pass and Sam got flushed out of the pocket. Who should be waiting but Tom Jackson.

Sam is a big guy, so he didn't really know how to slide. What he did on this play, unfortunately, was to lead with his face, and indecisively at that. Tom Jackson just drilled him.

By the time I got there to lend a hand, Sam was in a world of hurt. Tommy Jackson had jacked Sam's helmet around so far that Sam was looking out of the earhole. Sam straightened his helmet up and tried to talk. "Pffft, pfft, pfft," was all that came out. He eventually muttered about having something in his mouth.

Well, what he had in his mouth was his mustache. His tooth went right through his upper lip and pulled his mustache back inside with it. So Sam was trying to spit out his mustache after it had been yanked in through his split lip. He was bleeding and dizzy, but he managed to get to his feet. He didn't want to go out of the game.

Sam turned to the receivers and said, "Guys, you're going to have to run your routes to my right side because I can't see out of my left eye."

They literally told Zorn to tape an aspirin to whatever it was that knocked him out of the game. Dave Krieg was only a rookie third-stringer, and Sam was seeing in triplicate and he had his mustache inside his mouth. Jackson just killed him. Just drilled him right in the chops. But that was my roomie, Sam ... very tough but not very lucky!

The Rest of the Story

Tommy Jackson was a one-man wrecking crew that day. Before force-feeding Sam Adkins his own mustache, Jackson drove Jim Zorn into the Kingdome carpet with such force that the football nearly lodged in Jim's ribcage. Jimmy thought he broke every one of his ribs. He couldn't breathe, and the pain was just unbelievable.

So Jimmy came out of the game. Enter Sam Adkins. Enter Sam Adkins's mustache into his mouth.

Enter Dave Krieg, who couldn't find his rear end with both hands. They went in at the half and tried to give Jimmy a pain-killing shot, with comical results.

The needle they use for such things has to reach between the ribs and into the cartilage, so it's plenty long. And it hurts. The trick is jamming it in there far enough without poking through a lung.

The doctor stuck it in a first time, pulled it out, waited and ... nothing. He pushed it back in a second time, pulled it out, waited and ... still no relief. Right about then, Jimmy looked down at this needle sticking out of his ribs, and with the pain being so bad already, the poor guy blacked out. The doctor, thinking he'd just poked a hole in Jimmy's lung, started to get dizzy himself. And then he went down.

So the quarterback and the doctor were both passed out. Jimmy Whitesel, our trainer, had to revive them both. They somehow pulled their faculties together, but shot No. 3 was no more effective.

The doctor finally went all the way behind Z-man and stuck the needle in through his back. The pain started to subside, but it's a good thing the season was nearly over. Jim would have been unavailable for another six weeks, the pain was so bad. But he finished that game against the Broncos. Somehow, some way.

FIRST IMPRESSION:
Bob Newton

Joe Albi Stadium was in sad shape back when the Seahawks and Chicago Bears played a preseason game there in 1976. The rickety old venue is located in Spokane, some 300 miles from Seattle and a million more from the spacious Kingdome. Built in 1950 and later named for one of Spokane's most beloved civic leaders, Albi featured criminally unforgiving Astroturf, YMCA-caliber locker rooms and grandstands with room for a little over 30,000 captives. The big time it was not.

So here came the Bears with Walter Payton, most notably, and a veteran guard from Nebraska named Bob Newton. Bob was All-America for the Huskers in 1970, and he blocked for Johnny Rodgers, the 1972 Heisman Trophy winner. If venturing into Joe Albi seemed to mark a career low for Newton, the Bears had news for him. The team released him after the game and Seattle, desperate for talent heading into its inaugural season, snapped him up off waivers.

"My God, these guys play in that crappy stadium over in Spokane," a horrified Newton thought at the time, unaware that the team would play its home games in the Kingdome. "This is going to be the end of my career. Anybody but the Seahawks."

"Papa Fig," as he became known to his teammates, started for the next six years along Seattle's offensive front.

Mr. Raible, Meet Mr. Tatum

Ephren Hererra's 46-yard field goal on November 26, 1978 made Seattle the first team since 1965 to sweep the Oakland Raiders. That's what they tell me, anyway. I caught a touchdown pass in that game, and Jim Zorn still calls it the best corner route he ever threw.

But Jack Tatum, the Raiders' lovable safety, made sure I missed the postgame revelry. A little background is in order before we relive the hit that left me with a concussion whose effects lingered when I met my wife a short time later.

Back in those days, the sportswriters held a weekly luncheon at Gasperetti's Roma Café in Seattle's Pioneer Square. They would invite some local coach or athlete down and he'd tell a couple stories, they would ask some questions and that way they could all sit around and write a story without having to leave the lunch table. Not a bad deal at all.

Well, every team has players the reporters consider go-to guys, even after even the grisliest defeat. In those days, I was one of those guys.

Along the way, I was starting to get the idea that this whole talking in public thing was kind of fun, and I might just want to do some of this after the playing days were over. So I went down to Gasperetti's and I actually prepared a couple of remarks.

I would say something irreverent like, "You know, the organization is really great. We're treated like human beings and valuable contributing members. I remember, I was telling (GM) John Thompson just the other day when I was shining his shoes ..."

Well, somebody eventually asked me whether the Raiders would be "up" for this game, and I said something flip like, "With as many drugs as they take there, they're up all the time." I didn't know it at the time, but that little remark made it onto the bulletin board at the Raiders' locker room: "Seahawk Player Accuses Raiders of Taking Drugs."

So I catch a touchdown pass in that game, caught it behind Skip "Dr. Death" Thomas. If you're ever going to catch a touchdown pass on anybody with a nickname like Dr. Death, that's always a good thing.

But later in the game, on that drive to Efren's winning field goal, I cross the middle and the ball is a little behind me. I try to tip it back to myself, and Tatum just levels me. Hit me right in the earhole and just knocked me unconscious. Turns out they didn't call him The Assassin for nothing.

So we get back from Oakland and I spend the night in the hospital with wires attached to my head checking for a concussion.

But there's a happy ending to the story. I was invited to a dinner party that I had promised I'd go to the very next day, and I met my wife there. And I've often said that it was because of the brain injury that we met, and that was that.

Pain in the Thumb

W e were working on a trick play in practice back in the early days and the kick returner was supposed to lateral to defensive lineman Dennis Boyd, who would then wait for the coverage team to converge before unleashing a pass across the field to a speedier return man.

Dennis had thrown the javelin years earlier, so having him throw wasn't a stretch.

Well, just as Dennis went to throw, guard Ron Coder came barreling right at him on the coverage team. Never mind that we were out there in shorts, just trying to make sure guys were in the right places. Ron was going to make the play and be a hero. So he made this giant swat at the ball, only to miss and whack Dennis on the thumb. The bone came right out of the skin, sending a trail of blood along Dennis Boyd's arm as he held up his hand in agony.

As we recounted the story over at Jack Patera's house one day, Sam Adkins relayed what Dennis had told him later. What Patera said next caught us all off guard. It was vintage Jack ... gruff, tough and still blessed with a wicked sense of humor.

Sam: "Dennis played with the broken thumb the next day. As he watched film of the game later, he saw how he had subconsciously protected the thumb every time he made a tackle. He would go in and try to make the play and he'd be in position and then he'd put his hand behind his back to protect it and then try to make a play just one-handed."

Jack: "The wuss."

I'm pretty sure he was kidding. Jack knew better than anyone that football was a tough game played by tough guys, and Dennis Boyd was certainly one of those.

The Ol' Three-Day Plan

One guy interrupted a hunting trip somewhere in the hinterlands to come play on less than a week's notice. Another left each Friday from his job at a bank to serve as the long snapper on Sundays.

While some teams began lining up replacements weeks before the 1987 players strike, the Seahawks and others had been optimistic about a settlement. And so when the league said the games would go on, Seattle had less than a week to scrape together a team for its October 4 game against the Dolphins.

"I don't know what your biggest wins in Seahawk history were," former club vice president Randy Mueller said, "but those of us that were there a long time said our strike win against Miami in the Dome was one of the top four or five wins the franchise ever had."

General manager Mike McCormack managed to coax Bruce Mathison into the fold a couple days before kickoff, and the veteran passer came through with 326 yards and a clutch pass to Jimmy Teal on the winning drive. As for any evidence of such an outcome during the three practices leading up to the game? Forget it.

"Wednesday of that week, we were running the option," Mueller mused. "We were awful. It was the Bad News Bears."

Striking players heckled the replacements from beyond a fence that lined the practice field. Tight end Mike Tice could be as relentless as he was acerbic. The future Vikings coach saved some of his sharpest commentaries for Daryl Baines, the shady running back Mueller found while scouting the nearby Auburn Panthers semipro team.

"Hey Baines, does the team know you're smuggling tires out of there after practice?"

Ouch. Baines actually died a few years later of gunshot wounds he suffered while fleeing a crackhouse. Mueller escaped from that season mostly unscathed, although McCormack chewed him out for revealing to a reporter the ridiculous lengths the team was going to find players.

"You're going to make it look like we don't know what we're doing," McCormack warned.

"Hey, Mike, we don't," Randy thought. "You just told me to go to an Auburn Panther game. Come on."

Just Not as Often

Some of the veterans seemed more concerned with self-preservation than trying to beat Philadelphia at Veterans Stadium in the final game of our inaugural year.

Guys were telling me to protect my knees. This is what it's like to be a pro, I thought.

We lost, 27-10, and Coach Patera was livid afterward.

On the plane ride back to Seattle, Jack called five or six of the younger guys back for face-to-face chats. He was determined to make sure we knew what it took to be professionals. Sherman Smith, Steve Largent, Jim Zorn and I were among those Jack summoned to the seat he left open across the aisle.

Six preseason games and 14 regular-season games had seemed like three college seasons to me, but no matter. Jack wanted me back in Seattle as soon as possible.

"We want you around here for a while. You catch the ball just as well as Largent." Jack paused. "Just not as often."

Two Men, One Bed and a Stunned Coach

Andy MacDonald was in charge of bed check the night one of our receivers hopped into the sack with a mule.

This mule was actually Sam "Mule" Adkins, our backup quarterback and one of the funniest guys you'll ever meet. As for revealing the identity of the receiver in question, well, let's just say he works in broadcasting at the CBS affiliate in Seattle.

It was training camp in 1979 and we were feeling pretty good about ourselves. We had gone 9-7 the year before and pretty much everyone was back. We were having a good camp, too, but breaking up the monotony required some creativity.

We generally got back to the dorms around 10 each night and bed check was at 11, so there wasn't much time.

Well, Mule and I were roommates and we had decided early on that we were going to set up Andy, our running backs coach, before training camp was over. Andy was just a great guy. He was kind of high-strung, but very funny. He and his wife, Dolly, were just wonderful people. Andy was the perfect target.

Bed check was approaching, and so we locked the door, knowing Andy had a pass key. We could hear him knocking at the doors and checking rooms all the way down the hall and he was starting to get closer to our room.

So Sam and I put the plan into effect. And the plan was that we'd turn out the lights, and since we didn't have a candle or anything like that, we threw a shirt over the desk lamp. I wanted to turn the radio to one of those love music stations, but Cheney didn't have one of those, so I just found the farm report and turned it down real low.

And because it was Cheney and there was no air conditioning in the dorm, the last thing you needed was a blanket. You barely had a sheet and a pillow. I generally slept with no clothes on because it was cooler.

So we both get undressed and Sam gets into bed and then I get into the same bed with him. Now, a college dorm bed is not very big. It's not big enough for a regular-sized player anyway, let alone two guys.

Sam's ankles are hanging off the bed and he's of a wide girth anyway, so he's taking up most of the mattress. I kind of curl in next to him and sort of put my head on his chest.

We're lying there and we're just naked as jaybirds. And I hear the little knock at the door and Andy tries the doorknob and it's not open, so I know he's going to use the key. And the key goes in the doorknob and at that point, everything went into slow motion. It became like a Sam Peckinpah movie.

Andy MacDonald was used to seeing me in uniform.

The door slowly opened and Andy starts to step into the room.

Now, it's kind of dark because there's a T-shirt that is burning on a lamp nearby. And Andy starts to look over at Mule's bed and he doesn't see anybody. And so as his head starts to turn and his attention is turned back to the near bed and he goes, "OK, Adkins, where's …"

And he just kind of stops. And he sort of swallows the "where's"—it becomes woo-ooo-ooo-ooo. And he looks to the bed that we were on and you could see him counting to himself.

He's looking at the foot of the bed and he sees one-two feet, three-four feet. Then he sees four ankles and four knees and two … OH MY GOD! There's my head lying on Sam's chest, naked, and I look up to Andy and I say, "For heaven sakes, can we get a little privacy here, Andy?"

And he literally falls back against the door. He had his clipboard where he was checking names off the list, and he drops it. Papers fly everywhere.

He's a coach, he doesn't know what else to do, so he starts blowing his whistle. Coaches start running with fire axes. They think the building is burning down. And Andy, bless his heart, goes right back to Coach Patera and he tells him how we've got to break camp immediately because the players were going crazy in the dorms.

In some ways we were.

One Dead Cat Coming Right Up

The room was dark and its occupants asleep when a hulking figure rushed through the doorway, bent on a little chemical warfare. Bill Sandifer wasn't the first NFL player to enlist a fire extinguisher in a training-camp prank, but that was little consolation to a couple guys trying to get some shuteye.

The door flew open and all we could see was the silhouette of a figure in the doorway. Then all of a sudden, boom, off goes one of those dry chemical extinguishers that just fills the place with powder and sucks all the air out of the room. Sam Adkins and I came blasting out of our room coughing and covered with white powder.

This was the day before camp broke in 1978, so our suitcases were out and open with most everything packed. The backgammon board was still open and now everything had an inch of this awful powder on it.

I ran down the hall and there's a bunch of guys playing cards in one of the rooms, and I just go in there in an absolute rant. These guys must have thought I was insane. White dust is falling off of me and I'm standing in there screaming about how I'll kill these guys and I don't care who did it…me, a pencil-neck wide receiver threatening guys twice my size.

Sandifer, a defensive tackle from UCLA who spent two years with us, was one of the guys playing cards. I didn't know he was the guilty party, so I eventually started telling a few select guys that, hey, all I know is I'm of Italian descent and I know how my uncles would take care of this. I let it be known that when I found out who it was, somebody was going to find a dead cat nailed to his front door.

Well, word started getting around and probably two weeks later, Sandifer comes up and he says, "All right, listen, I don't want to find any damn cat on my door. I've got two young kids and I don't want to scare them. I apologize. I'll pay for your dry cleaning, whatever."

He kind of felt bad about it, but he felt worse about the cat. Of course, I would never hurt a cat, but Bill didn't have to know that.

Heart Only Goes So Far

I f nothing else, that 35-9 loss to the Browns in the 1994 finale produced one of the better postgame quotes, courtesy of offensive coordinator Larry Kennan.

"Defensively, we were starting a guy (Dion Lambert) who didn't get here until Tuesday. It's difficult. They had a lot of emotion at the Alamo, but their asses got whipped, too, because they were outmanned. That's what we were today."

Can't Say We Didn't Have a Shot

C oach Patera was a stickler for not arriving at the stadium too early. He didn't like people sitting around the locker room. He figured you'd get stiff, get nervous, start worrying, whatever.

He wanted everybody to show up an hour and a half before the game, get dressed, go out to warmups and then play.

But if you were hurt, then you had to get to the stadium earlier for special tapings.

Before that 1980 game in Dallas, there were actually more people in the locker room for the special tapings than came on the final bus, where most of the players were supposed to be.

Merlin Olson was doing the game that day on TV with Dick Enberg, and I knew Merlin a little bit. He knew I was interested in the TV business. And so he was talking about how many guys we had hurt, and I offered to give him a first-hand look inside the training room.

Coach Patera wasn't there, and happily so, because he didn't like any "outsiders" in there. We walked in and there was a table lined up with all the needles. There must have been 15 needles marked with names of guys who were going to get shot before this game.

I had one for my ankle or shoulder or something. But there were a whole bunch of them. Merlin let out an audible groan. He knew we were in trouble that day. People told me later that he wasn't making excuses for us during the broadcast, but he made a point of telling viewers they weren't seeing the real Seahawks, and how Dallas was one of the great teams of the decade.

It's not fair sometimes, but like Mike Holmgren often says, nobody cares if you're hurt. That's just the way it goes.

FIRST IMPRESSION:
The Kingdome

I'll never forget walking into the Kingdome for the first time. And then that first game ... the place was packed and rocking. We lost to St. Louis in that opening game, but the atmosphere was electric. "This really is the big time," I remember thinking.

Got to Look Up, Rook

I was not the bravest person in the world, and I did have a sincere concern about crossing the middle on a guy like Jack Tatum. But then at times you're kind of unaware, you're just thinking about going out there to play the game. You don't think of some of these things.

We played in Pittsburgh one year and my folks came up from Kentucky to watch. And I ran an underneath crossing route from the slot position and Jack Lambert was in the middle.

Lambert acts like he doesn't see me coming, and as I'm crossing behind him, he just swings this arm around and catches me right in the throat as I'm running by. He had all that tape and padding on those arms and he could really unload.

So, for the rest of the game, I can barely talk. Afterward, my dad says, "Well, boy, he really hit you, didn't he?" And it's all I can do to get the words out. "Thanks Dad. Hey, how ya doing?"

And Dad is laughing. "Boy, he really knocked the crap out of you, didn't he? He's a hell of a player, that Lambert." Again, I can barely talk. I'm whispering. "Yeah, Dad, he really is."

They say to get your head on a swivel and by gosh, you do. You grow up in a hurry.

My rookie year, 1976, cornerback Pat Fisher taught me a lesson. We were playing the Redskins and Fisher, one of the smallest players in the league, didn't seem to merit much concern from me.

So, the first play I get out there, I line up in a three-point stance and I'm looking in toward the ball, like we always did. The ball is snapped and before I can even turn my head to look up, this little tiny guy, Pat Fisher, comes up and cold-cocks me. Knocks me *on my butt*.

"Got to look up, rook," he told me. "Better know who you're playing against out here, rook."

Then he walks back to the huddle and I'm dizzy. I spent more of my time dizzy from somebody cold-cocking me because I just wasn't aware. You really do learn in a hurry.

When I have headaches today, or I forget what I was just talking about, well, that's one of the reasons.

Anyone Got a Light?

A knee injury derailed my senior season at Georgia Tech, so the Packers wanted to bring me in for an examination heading into the draft.

I flew into Green Bay and had lunch with Bart Starr, who was coaching the team at the time. Of course, this was heady stuff for a kid who grew up rooting for Paul Hornung, Jimmy Taylor and those guys.

We went into the locker room at Lambeau Field and I was stunned by what I saw: ashtrays attached to each locker.

As Bart Starr explained, "Only men play this game, Steve."

Yeah, men, but smoking in the locker room?

Sweating Bullets

O ur date with Dallas on Thanksgiving Day 1980 marked our third game in 11 days. We played on Monday, Sunday and Thursday, so it was unbelievable. We had so many guys hurt.

And the Cowboys were a pretty fair team at the time. So we're getting beat out there pretty good and guys are just banged up and they're carrying people off the field. It looks like a battlefield, the Civil War: Here comes several wagons pulled by horses with four or five more Seahawks on the back.

Somehow, Rusty Tillman and I got into a thing when he was special teams coach where we were always doing impressions of the old vaudeville entertainer Georgie Jessel, whose sing-songy nasal delivery was a staple on *The Tonight Show.*

So we're on the sideline against Dallas and we're getting our fannies handed to us and we go directly into Georgie Jessel mode while discussing the upcoming punt return.

"Saaaaay, what do you want," I say to Rusty, "middle return or a right return?"

And Rusty would say, as though responding to Johnny Carson, "Johhhhn, let's go middle return, but remember, we're getting our asses killed, so don't try to get it all back in one play."

And I almost fell down. And as soon as I start laughing, Coach Patera looks over. I almost swallowed my entire mustache, facemask and everything trying to make sure Jack didn't see me laughing. And Rusty had his back to him, so Jack couldn't see Rusty.

I'm sweating bullets. I had always been known as a guy who worked hard and all that stuff, and here I am laughing at Georgie Jessel on the sideline. We're getting hammered on national TV, and I'm going to get cut the next day, I was sure.

I could just hear Jack saying, "Men, we don't laugh on the sidelines when we're getting beat like that, and that's why I cut Steve Raible." The whole way back from Dallas I could just see it coming. Unbelievable.

CHAPTER 4

Turbulence Ahead

S ay what you want about Dennis Erickson, but give him this: He's a survivor. Almost nothing went right during his four years as head coach, and yet for most of that time, Dennis soldiered ahead without showing cracks on the exterior.

The list of calamities and distractions included but was not limited to:

• a car crash that left defensive lineman Mike Frier paralyzed;

- a DUI conviction that resulted in Dennis attending AA meetings;
- a bungled attempt to move the franchise to Southern California, during which time Dennis worked out of a Residence Inn;
- learning about a change in ownership on the morning of the NFL draft;
- a virtual monsoon that helped doom the Hawks to a crushing defeat in Kansas City;
- and the notorious Vinny Testaverde phantom touchdown that helped bring back instant replay (but only after Seattle had lost a critical game and Dennis had lost his job).

"He was as flexible and as accommodating as I've ever seen and maybe that's a negative, I don't know," one former co-worker said. "But I know this: He handled more (stuff) better than anybody that I've seen. It was water off a duck's back.

"If the things that happened to Dennis would have happened to anybody else, there would have been major repercussions. Could you imagine Chuck Knox or Mike Holmgren putting up with that? They'd be looking to choke somebody. Dennis would just roll with the punches."

Just Wait Until We Lose

Dennis Erickson once filled out a questionnaire asking what job he might hold were it not for football. The question stumped him. Dennis had never considered anything else. When the Seahawks presented him with one of the BMWs they provided to head coaches, Dennis couldn't figure out how to release the trunk.

If it didn't have to do with football, Dennis was lost. He's a coach through and through, and also a guy without much pretense.

Those qualities helped Dennis win big at Miami and Oregon State. They hurt him during his first public-speaking engagement as Seahawks coach. A schmoozer, Dennis was not.

We were at a Sea Hawkers' fan-club banquet and I was emceeing. What probably should have been a slam dunk was actually a bit awkward.

"Ladies and gentlemen, without further ado, the new head coach of the Seattle Seahawks, Dennis Erickson!"

The place went nuts. Dennis had grown up near Seattle and he came to the Seahawks with considerable fanfare. The Sea Hawkers gave him a standing ovation, but Dennis didn't seem comfortable in the spotlight.

"You're standing up and clapping now," he said, "but wait until I lose a few games. We'll see if you're still cheering."

That was one of the first comments from Dennis Erickson as Seahawks head coach. I'd forgotten those remarks, but my wife Sharon remembered them. She thought that was kind of strange. She considered it to be almost foretelling.

Dennis went on to talk about other things, but not for long. Get him talking about friends or family and there wasn't anyone more congenial. But when it came to football, Dennis was a coach, not a salesman. As the franchise struggled through some rocky years, a little more schmoozability might have served him well. But that just wasn't Dennis.

One on One with Dennis

Dennis Erickson was a tough guy to get to know. I felt pretty good about our relationship and I always felt that he was forthright and honest with me.

I remember when they locked up the building and said they were going to move the franchise to California. People on the staff were saying it's going to happen, the owner is going to close down the shop and he's going to move us all to California.

This was 1996. It was just rumor at that time, but I had people who were confirming it for me. So we went with it at KIRO-TV and a few days later, I got a call from Dennis's secretary. They weren't doing any interviews, but I got on the phone with Dennis and he said, "Look, I know you guys want to do an interview. I'll talk to you."

Well, they put up the fences all around the facility and they locked up all the gates. And here I come walking up and all these people are standing outside the gate waiting to get in, and I just walk right through with a camera crew and they lock the gate behind. You could just hear the mumbling and the grumbling going on.

We sat down to talk and for Dennis, it was, "Look, I'm an employee here. I don't own this team. This guy wants to win and he feels like this is what it's going to take. But, yes, this is a bit of a distraction and sure, I came home to coach here. This is the reason I took this job, to come home, and now it looks like they're going to move us to California."

It didn't last that long, but it was kind of tough on him.

It wasn't as tough on players. They get traded, they get cut, they go places. They play. For coaches, anything that's cause for uncertainty makes it difficult.

But I always got along pretty well with Dennis.

Heading South

Attempts to relocate the franchise to Southern California in 1996 created hardships for all involved. Owner Ken Behring set up the team at the Los Angeles Rams' old headquarters, which had been an elementary school.

With free agency upon them, Seahawks execs Mickey Loomis and Randy Mueller actually formulated their off-season plan in the parking lot. They somehow managed to re-sign Michael Sinclair and Dean Wells while landing free agent safety Darryl Williams.

"We never thought we'd have a chance to sign any of them because we couldn't even tell them where we were going to play," Mueller said. "We were staying at a Residence Inn and working out at Ram Park while they were renovating it."

The league forced the Seahawks back to Seattle. Behring eventually sold the team to current owner Paul Allen. Sinclair went on to lead the league with 16.5 sacks in 1998, while Wells and Williams were productive starters.

Paging Steve Broussard

One long-time Seahawks official was sweating bullets as he approached the practice field with some bad news. The league had taken issue with Steve Broussard's new contract. The running back would have to leave practice until the clause in question could be re-worked.

Interfering with an NFL practice is a risky proposition. Coaches tend to resemble short-fused dictators as they venture to keep 50-some-odd players on task for two hours.

And so it was with caution that the official approached new coach Dennis Erickson.

"I didn't know what he was going to do. This was after nearly 10 years with Chuck. I'm like, yeah, I'm going to take this guy off the field? I remember going out and telling Dennis during practice, kind of on the side where no one could see."

A nonchalant Erickson defused any fears of a blowup. "What are you telling me for? Get him out of here."

Only worry about what you can control. That was Dennis.

Whitecaps in Kansas City

The aisles at Arrowhead Stadium resembled the elaborate water features found at an over-the-top Las Vegas hotel. Rainwater cascaded down onto the field, where whitecaps actually washed over the players' ankles. Worse for the 1998 Seahawks and coach Dennis Erickson, starting quarterback Warren Moon left the game with broken ribs.

Up in the press box, water broke through the ceiling, shorting out overhead TV monitors. Bill Williamson, then the Seahawks beat reporter for the *Everett Herald*, hurriedly moved his laptop to dry ground as the drips turned to a steady stream.

Inside Seattle's owners box, league officials asked Seahawks vice president Randy Mueller to find out whether Erickson wanted to continue the Sunday night game. And so down went Mueller, first to the locker room, where he changed into boots and assorted SCUBA gear, and then onto the Seahawks' shoreline for an interview with the skipper.

"You'd think you were playing at Lake Erie," Mueller said. "And we're trying to talk on the sidelines. Dennis is going, 'Hold on a second, I've got to call a play here.' And we're trying to decide what to do with the team. Do we stay? Do we want to reschedule?"

Dennis simply wanted to come up for air. "Here's the deal: Just get me out of here. Get us all out of here. This is miserable."

Of course, by the time Randy made it back upstairs with the message, the rain had pretty much stopped. NFL brass decided to play the game after an extended delay. Seattle lost, 17-6, and Dennis lost his quarterback too. The season was sinking fast.

Phantom Touchdown
Haunts Hawks

The water-logged 1998 loss in Kansas City was the second of three consecutive defeats following a 3-0 start to the season. Warren Moon's broken ribs remained a problem as the Seahawks dipped further to 5-6, but backup Jon Kitna got them back to .500 with a clutch performance during a 20-18 home win over Tennessee.

Seattle trailed 18-17 with 27 seconds left when Kitna led them into position for Todd Peterson's winning 48-yard field goal.

"That was the spark that I think we needed," safety Mark Collins said. "Hopefully we can build on that. This thing is far from over."

And so the Seahawks took a 6-6 record, along with some renewed optimism, into the Meadowlands for a must-win game against the Jets. Kitna was up to the task. He completed 17 of 24 passes for 278 yards, replete with 70- and 57-yard scoring strikes to Joey Galloway, as the Seahawks closed in on victory.

The outcome seemed secure when safety Jay Bellamy tackled Jets quarterback Vinny Testaverde short of the goal line on the game's final play. And then the unthinkable happened: Linesman Earnest Frantz III signaled touchdown from some 25 yards away, somehow mistaking Testaverde's helmet for the football.

Jets 32, Seahawks 31. The NFL's head of officiating called Erickson to apologize the next day, but the damage was done. While players spoke out against the absurdity of the error, Erickson held his tongue. He even joked about needing to avoid an NFL fine because his wife had big plans for the holiday shopping season.

"I don't know if I feel snakebit," Dennis said in the wake of that loss, "but obviously it's very frustrating to be close and to play well and to not get to that next level. We were very close to doing that and yesterday would have been a big step for us. And it didn't happen."

The Seahawks won their next two, but lost at Denver to close the season. Their 8-8 record sealed Erickson's fate. He was fired a day after the season.

Prayed Upon

W arren Moon and tight end Deems May conducted a little investigation after a series of slow starts hurt the Seahawks in 1997. The two veterans sniffed out a pregame prayer ring. Some 20 guys were meeting in the shower for prayer sessions after the team came off the field following pregame warmups.

The prayers seemed to be leaving some players in a reflective mood just as kickoff approached.

"When you come out of that locker room, you should be on fire, ready to play," Moon said. "So many times guys were coming out contemplative. They'd been thinking and praying. Instead of being ready to go out and kill somebody, you come out in a more relaxed state than when you went in."

Dennis Erickson agreed. He moved the prayer sessions to before warmups. The slow starts went away almost instantly.

"We had a lot of guys who prayed on that team," Erickson quipped years later. "By the end of the year I was praying to keep my job."

Almost Great in '98

That '98 team had a chance to be special. Those guys opened the season with a 38-0 shellacking of the Eagles in Philly. They were 3-1 heading into Kansas City, but it didn't last.

With Warren either slowed or out of the lineup altogether, the offense just wasn't the same. Jon Kitna made strides late in the year, but he was still a few years away from blossoming into the Pro Bowl-caliber guy the Bengals came to love in 2003.

That offense was strong with Walter Jones and House Ballard at tackle, Pete Kendall at guard, Warren and Ricky and Steve Broussard in the backfield and Joey Galloway stretching defenses on the outside. People forget that Joey had more catches for more yards and more touchdowns in his first four years than anyone in franchise history, Largent included. He could break open a game on punt returns, too.

The defense was stacked with talent, but a bit flighty and undependable against the run in particular. Linebackers coach Jim Johnson had those guys stirred into a frenzy with all those creative blitz packages, leading to eight interception returns for touchdowns and 10 defensive TDs overall.

Michael Sinclair, Cortez Kennedy, Sam Adams and Phillip Daniels caused problems up front. Darryl Williams was a Pro Bowl safety. Shawn Springs was healthy and dominating from his left corner position.

Chad Brown was an irrepressible force at linebacker and Darrin Smith was a play-maker, too, at least until he pulled a hammy high-stepping into the end zone on a play that reduced John Elway to befuddled admirer ("That was something I haven't seen in 16 years, when the soft-side linebacker picks off a weak-side hook," Elway marveled. "I'm giving the credit to Darrin. He made a great, great play. If I had to do it again, I'd throw the same play, the same pass I threw. He just made a great play.")

Darrin's amazing pick should've been enough to win at home, but the offense didn't do its part. Warren gutted it out, but the ribs were a major factor in his 15-of-32 performance that day. The defense, desperate to force a turnover, instead gave up a 70-yard run to Terrell Davis in the late stages.

"If Warren wouldn't have gotten hurt, that team was a really good team," Springs said. "We could have won the Super Bowl that year."

CHAPTER 5

1983 Cinderella Season

The 1982 players' strike brought together many guys like nothing else ever did. The Seahawks had won a couple of games at the end of that season after general manager Mike McCormack came in as coach and got the players excited about winning again.

Then Chuck Knox came in and signed a few veterans like Charle Young, Cullen Bryant, Robert Pratt, Reggie McKenzie and Blair Bush. These were guys who had some experience and knew how to win. He changed enough of the chemistry to make it his team.

Jacob Green always liked Jack Patera. But it wasn't until Chuck brought in some of those veterans that the team learned how to come together on both sides of the ball. Chuck's teams developed a closeness that would be hard to duplicate in today's game.

"We got Blair Bush very quickly because I determined we were going to have a center, somebody who could play. And of course Reggie McKenzie would bring the toughness and he had played for us with the Bills and that would cement that position. And Pratt was the same way."

But perhaps more than people realize, Chuck won that first season with a lot of Jack Patera's guys. And then, of course, they traded up in the draft to take Curt Warner. Even then, it took some time.

Obscure Beginnings

The Cinderella Seahawks were middling along at 4-4 when the head coach inched closer to a fateful decision. Chuck felt the team needed a spark. It was Week 10 when he handed over the offense to a 25-year-old Dave Krieg. NFL Films was there.

"This guy is a young guy, but he's got a strong arm, he's got great vision, he's got a charisma. He's kind of a street fighter kind of guy. He's unselfish and he's a leader in the huddle. He just needs to play. He's young and he needs to play," noted Chuck.

And Dave was sitting there being interviewed as well, and he had this almost pageboy-looking haircut. His mission was clear.

"If I don't know what I'm doing, I'm not letting my teammates know that. I'll fool them somehow."

Krieg fooled them, all right, as did his team. There was nothing particularly pretty about the 1983 Seahawks, not statistically anyway. The defense allowed more yards (6,029) than any in franchise history, eclipsed only when the 2000 team gave up 6,391. The offense was potent but also had its limitations. Even the regular-season record (9-7) had already been achieved twice in the four non-strike seasons since the league adopted a 16-game schedule in 1978.

And yet those '83 Hawks willed their way deeper into the playoffs than any Seattle team before or since. They led the AFC in takeaways. And with Rusty Tillman infusing his energy into the special teams, Seattle became the second NFL team to lead the league in both punt and kick coverage. There were also two touchdowns on kick returns and a third via punt return.

It's kind of funny. Even though Jack Patera obviously preached playing good defense and special teams for all those years, nobody really knew anything about that when it came to our team. All they knew about was our offense: Jim Zorn's ability to scramble and throw, Steve Largent's ability to make these incredible catches.

But it took Chuck Knox only one season to truly convince this team that the way you win a championship is through good defense, good special teams, avoiding mistakes and being able to run the ball, especially come crunch time. Some teams need several years to learn that, and maybe that was the most amazing thing about that '83 team. They learned it so quickly and they learned it so well from Knox that they got all the way to the AFC championship game.

Changing of the Guard

Jim Zorn glanced toward the sideline through the corner of one eye, just in time to see the new head coach spike his hat to the ground in disgust. Chuck Knox was furious, and he was running out of patience. Dave Krieg would be the quarterback before long.

"I could feel during the '83 season that we were just playing average football," Jim said. "I just had a sense they were waiting for me to do something so they could put Dave in there."

They wouldn't have to wait any longer than halftime of the Pittsburgh game in Week 8. The Steelers were already in control when Jim delivered a ball into the ground three yards short of a wide-open Curt Warner. It had been third and seven, but for Jim it seemed like fourth and forever.

"I just felt like the whole weight of the team and every mistake that had ever been made by the team over the years was on my shoulders. I just felt terrible. I could almost feel the end coming."

As they came out for the second half, down 24-0, quarterbacks coach Kenny Meyer gave Jim the news. That was pretty much the end for Jim, and a painful one at that.

"It was a lot more difficult being demoted than being cut. Being cut, you can go someplace and get a new start. But being demoted, you have to buck up and be a team guy, but also know that everything you did for the franchise over the years doesn't matter any more."

Mudbone to the Rescue

It started in the second half of that Pittsburgh game on October 23. The Hawks found themselves down 24-0 when Chuck turned to Dave Krieg to start the second half. And that's when the '83 team discovered it had a playmaker at quarterback. Not that Jimmy couldn't make plays. There was just something about Dave Krieg. His time had come.

Dave gave that team a street-fighter kind of guy under center, an unselfish player and a leader in the huddle. His teammates saw that, especially in that game against the Steelers. With Dave at the controls, the Seahawks stormed back to make it close, falling 27-21.

Dave had that attitude, that cockiness. The Seahawks beat the Jets the next week, and you could just feel the confidence growing.

By the time the AFC playoff game in Miami rolled around, the Seahawks knew they could win. They went in at halftime, in the Orange Bowl, and the intensity was higher than ever before.

There was a sense in the locker room that this team could win that game, that these players deserved to win that game, that they would find a way to win that game. And they did.

KC Shootout

Six weeks after a 38-36 decision over the Raiders, that '83 team prevailed in a 51-48 overtime shootout with the Chiefs. Norm Johnson's field goal won it, but a little razzle-dazzle helped.

Dave Krieg handed off the ball to Steve Largent from the shotgun formation, then released downfield as an eligible receiver.

"The ball was high," Chuck Knox said, "but he made a great acrobatic catch that kept the drive alive."

The play was good for 11 yards. The win helped Seattle get to 9-7 and into the playoffs.

No Holds Barred (Except One)

Credit Jacob Green for getting those '83 Hawks into the playoffs. It was a team effort, of course, but Jacob drew the crucial holding penalty that helped beat the Giants in a December road game the Seahawks had to have. The Hawks were 7-7 entering that game, which helped send them on their way to a 9-7 finish.

Jacob was being held even more than usual in this game, and he wasn't getting any calls. The Seahawks had the far superior team, but the Giants, in their first season under Bill Parcells, were scrappy and potentially dangerous at home.

And when Jeff Rutledge tossed a 10-yard TD pass to Earnest Gray with 25 seconds on the clock, the Giants appeared headed to only their fourth win in 15 tries that season. It wasn't to be. The points came off the board when referee Jerry Markbreit flagged right tackle John Tautolo for basically wrestling Jacob to the ground.

The penalty backed the Giants into a fourth-and-17 from the 20. Rutledge fired the ball to Byron Williams at the 2, but Williams had no chance. Kerry Justin and Keith Simpson drilled him as the ball arrived.

"That's the game I remember from that '83 season," Jacob said. "Don't get me wrong, that playoff win in Miami was great, but we don't get there if we don't win that game against the Giants."

Parcells questioned the holding call immediately following the game, only to relent after watching the film a day later. Tautolo also proved to be a standup guy in comments that appeared in the *New York Times*: "I kind of thought I held. I grabbed him and threw him down, but I was doing that all game and they didn't call anything."

It Was How They Played the Game

The record was only 9-7. Hell, we'd had those two other times under Jack. But it was how they did it. It was with Chuck coaching and Curt Warner running the ball. It was a different offense, it was a different defense, but the same players with a couple of exceptions.

"We made a change at quarterback with David Krieg," Chuck reflected. "He came on and had just a fantastic season. We had drafted Curt Warner and that gave us a running back who could do some things.

"The defense played better as we went along and got a little confidence. We just had great attitude and everything, and we won some big games. A big game was beating the Giants in New York to go 9-7 and that put us in the playoff."

Curt had just a dynamite rookie year. We can safely call that 1,449-yard debut the single best rookie season of any player in team history. But the rest of the team was largely the same, personnel-wise, as the '82 team that stumbled through the strike year at 4-5.

Of course, teams are sometimes ripe for making a move like that. We've seen it in recent years with teams like Carolina, New England, and St. Louis. They have a lot of the pieces in place and it just takes somebody new to come in and get players to catch on. Maybe you say the same things in a little bit different way.

And they figure out, suddenly, that you can win. And then once you get them on a roll, then you have that little run in there. That's what Chuck had in the mid-80s and it all started with that unexpected rally through the '83 season.

Curtain Call

They controlled their own destiny going into the last game of the regular season, against the Patriots. And they won that final game by a 24-6 count. Perhaps even more revealing than the win was how the team and its fans celebrated the moment.

Here were a bunch of guys and a coach who had been together just one season. They had locked up a playoff berth, and they went into the locker room and they cheered and high-fived and all that stuff.

And then they did something that simply doesn't happen in football. They all came back out onto the field for a curtain call. Some guys came out with their shoulder pads still on. Other guys came out in T-shirts. And the fans were just going nuts in the Kingdome.

Had it been the last game ever in the Kingdome, or had the team played its final home game of the season, maybe that sort of thing happens. But these guys came back out and took a curtain call after earning the right to come back for a game against Denver a mere seven days later. Seattle's first whiff of the playoffs smelled that sweet.

"The crowd made so much noise and my security man had said we'd better come back out," Chuck Knox said. "We had guys with their shirts off and everything else going back out for a curtain call, a victory call."

Those Kingdome fans cheered with the same kind of emotion that Knox's teams showed on the field. Chuck wouldn't have it any other way.

"We were an emotional football team. We prided ourselves every week that we were going to battle hard and you were going to have to earn it if you were going to beat us. We came to play. And we celebrated that way."

Getting Hot

Dave Krieg completed 12 of 13 passes with three touchdowns in that first-round game, and Tom Catlin's defense just pounded the Broncos into submission. But that 31-7 win wasn't a surprise. Denver managed only 302 points that season, fewest by far in the five-team AFC West, and future comeback king John Elway was safely on the Denver sideline until the game was out of reach.

Upsetting Miami in the Orange Bowl was a different story. I remember the game very clearly. The Seahawks were leading in the fourth quarter, 17-13, and the offense was on its own 20- or 30-yard line. Well, Dave throws what he thought was going to be like a quick out to Largent, except Largent ran a quick slant. Dave threw the ball and the cornerback was the only person that was anywhere near the ball. He picked off the pass and the Dolphins went ahead soon thereafter.

It's funny because the NFL Films production had the audio from the radio call on there. I watched that again for the first time in years and it was me on the radio saying,

"This is the entire season resting on this next drive. Now let's see if this interception has affected him. I don't think it will. I think Krieg and the entire Seahawk offense are going to come out and move the ball down the field. Let's see what happens."

Well, sure enough, every now and then a blind squirrel finds the nut. Krieg completed two big passes to Largent, one of which got them down inside the 5. And then Curt Warner went around the right side for the touchdown that put them in the AFC championship game.

Taking the Family

Chuck Knox promised to expand the travel list for that playoff trip to Miami. "I had told the people who worked in our office at the Seahawks that if we win (in the first round), we'll take everybody. So, we had to get a bigger plane. We left on a Friday because I believed when you're going across the country, if you have a malfunction or whatever happens, we'll have time to make the adjustments. Sure enough, the black box that came in this very aircraft wasn't on the plane.

"So now we're going to have about a four-hour delay. I had a meeting at 9 a.m. in Miami scheduled at the Orange Bowl. Now right away they say, 'Coach, what are we going to do?' And I told them we were going to play the hand we're dealt, I don't want anyone talking about it, we're never going to use this as an excuse.

"We didn't get to the hotel until 5 a.m. on Saturday morning. I told the guys to just get a little sack time, take a shower, we're headed to the Orange Bowl at 8:30. I said you'll have all afternoon to sleep."

They got to the Orange Bowl, all right, but the field was covered. No one on the grounds crew spoke English. It wasn't looking good, but Chuck managed to make things work. He was always prepared.

What It's All About

Chuck Knox still gets emotional thinking about getting carried off the field following that win at the Orange Bowl.

"That was just wonderful. And the locker room was wonderful. Those guys, they were just really great. They gave me the game ball, which brought me to tears. I mean, that's what makes coaching worthwhile. They were going 'Chuck, Chuck, Chuck.' It's a wonderful feeling."

The Key to the City

Seattle's love affair with its NFL franchise began in '76, but expectations were minimal in those early years. As a young team that won some games, we could do no wrong.

The players' strike of '82 changed things for the fans. The subsequent firing of coach Jack Patera confirmed that football was a bottom-line business, even in Seattle.

That '83 team restored the magic, and then some. Long before Seattle fell for the '95 Mariners, there were those '83 Hawks.

Thousands of fans greeted them as the team returned from that playoff upset in Miami. Players encountered a mob scene as they came through that upper concourse

Dave Krieg, looking stylish in his 1983 Playoffs pull-over, greets fans at the Seattle airport after beating the Dolphins in Miami.

area. There were so many people and so many cars that getting out of the parking garage took two hours.

Third Time's No Charm

Beating the Dolphins secured a trip to Los Angeles for the AFC title game with the Raiders. Seattle had already swept the Raiders by scores of 38-36 at home and 34-21 on the road. But you know what they say about beating a team three times in one season. It's tough.

The Raiders won that game and went on to beat the Redskins in the Super Bowl.

Chuck Knox revels in the win that vaulted Seattle into its first and only AFC championship game.

Riot Gear, Anyone?

Our trip to Los Angeles for the 1983 AFC title game ended with an absolute riot on the field. Instead of doing a postgame interview with guests like we normally do, we just kept it there and we did a play by play over a riot. A lot of drunken fans had come right out of the stands to tear down the goalposts.

They had LAPD choppers and police on horseback and this army of police officers and yellow-coated security people, but these weren't just any fans. I mean, the fights were incredible. Unbelievable. They were just beating the tar out of each other.

So the police came down on horseback all the way across the field, backed by air support from the helicopters, and they just pushed everybody right off the floor of the stadium. It was something. That was a true riot out there.

At least we were upstairs. The easiest route from the press box to the locker room was directly down through the stands to the track, then back up through the tunnel. Happily, by the time we got done on the air they had cleared out the stands. Otherwise we were liable to get killed just walking down the stands.

That was always one of the great pastimes at the Coliseum, to scan around and find the fights because there were dozens of brawls in that stadium when we were down there.

And it wasn't Seahawks fans and Raiders fans. It was just Raiders fans beating the hell out of each other. You really didn't want to take the chance of getting killed down there.

CHAPTER 6

You Don't Know Jack

The memories came flooding back as Sam Adkins, Mike Sando and I made the 80-mile drive from Seattle over Snoqualmie Pass to rural Cle Elum. Loaded up with ample eats and a case of MGD, we gathered at the place where Jack Patera has settled in retirement. The Seahawks' first head coach is in his 80s now, still larger than life north of 300 pounds.

Jack devotes his time these days to the hunting dogs he raises on a modest 10-acre spread. On this day, the humor, good cheer and unforgettable stories flowed almost as freely

Jack Patera drives his point home after venturing well onto the field in the Kingdome.

as the scotch Jack went through. The fiery temperament that served the Seahawks well in the early days was nowhere to be found, having vanished with the demands of NFL life. Jack keeps his own schedule.

All these years later, people remember him for the wrong reasons. Jack Patera was so much more than a tough guy who wouldn't let his players have water during two-a-days. Outsiders rarely saw his terrific sense of humor or the reasons behind the things he did. Jack remains a quintessential character and a misunderstood one, at that.

Mr. Tolerance

We'll tolerate you until we can replace you. Those were Jack Patera's first words to the team on that first day of training camp in 1976.

The guys who had played for other teams seemed perplexed. What the hell was this? Who was this guy? Those of us who had never played pro football before were scared to death.

But, as it turned out, Jack was right on the money. Most coaches don't quite put it that way, but that's the way it was. When you think about those days before free agency, they did indeed use you until they could get rid of you, and you had no choice in the matter. You couldn't go anywhere. You could play for the them or get cut, and then perhaps you might catch on with somebody else.

So, yes, they tolerated you until they could replace you.

I've come to learn that Jack actually heard that for the first time when he was playing in Baltimore. He wasn't necessarily opening our eyes to this hard-hearted business where we were only pieces of meat. He was simply explaining that this was a tough job and you've got to work hard to keep your job, and eventually, you'll be replaced because guys are going to come in who are faster and stronger and bigger. He wanted us to know that each of us had an opportunity to make a place for himself on an NFL team, and that there weren't many people who could say that.

The older veterans, like John Demarie, Fred Hoaglin and Mike Curtis, liked Jack. To them, this guy was shooting straight, telling them the way it was. They knew they were only going to be Seahawks for a short time as veteran-allocation guys, because the team was going to be built on the draft, just as the winning franchises of the era were, the Dallases and the Minnesotas.

And those who really knew Jack, guys like Bob Lurtsema, who played for him back in Minnesota, those guys saw through the bluster. They knew how to pull Jack's chain a little bit and make him laugh. Jack could be a very funny guy.

Steak and Eggs

In the early days our pregame meals consisted of a 10-ounce New York strip steak and a pile of scrambled eggs. It took me about a season before it finally dawned on me that eating all this meat before a game was really not very smart.

After the first couple of years, a few of us went to Jack with a few menu suggestions.

"Hey, Jack, you know, actually, like French toast or maybe even pancakes might be better because they offer quicker energy. That meat just sort of sits there in your stomach."

And proving that Jack could be flexible, in the future we ate French toast and things like that. Probably saved the team money in the long run, too.

Sharp-Dressed Men

We wore coats and ties on the road because those were the rules according to Jack. That meant we wore them from the time we got out of our cars at the airport in Seattle to being on the plane ... to arriving at a city to going into the hotel lobby to going upstairs to our rooms.

We could take them off in the rooms, but that was about it. When you came downstairs, if you were going to visit family, if you were going to the pregame meal, if you were going out front from the lobby to grab a newspaper, you wore your tie. Jack didn't want to see people lounging around the lobby in sweats and cutoffs. These were business trips and we were to dress like businesspeople.

Anyway, the last game of the 1976 season rolled around and we were back in Philadelphia to play the Eagles. We practiced at Brown University on Saturday because the Vet wasn't available.

Well, Bob Lurtsema knew Jack real well, and Lurtsy was a funny guy anyway. He was a big defensive tackle who played behind the Purple People Eaters when Jack was the Vikings' d-line coach.

Anyway, Lurtsy convinced us all to bring our ties to practice. So here comes Jack walking out as we're stretching, and we all pull out these ties just about in unison. We put them on with our sweats.

And Jack loved it. He laughed and thought it was great. But the good cheer didn't last long.

Right in the midst of all this fun and laughter, Jack found out that our equipment manager, Harry Yalacki, forgot to bring the footballs to practice. So here we were out there at a football practice with ties but no balls. Jack went from laughing to being not the happiest person in the world at that moment. He was so organized, and then to have that happen ... man, he was hot. And Jack could climb on people. He could be merciless on a guy.

Poor Harry. That was the last game he ever did for the Seahawks. He was gone before the beginning of the second season.

I guess they tolerated him until they could replace him.

Blame It on the Balls

H arry Yalacki was a retired navy guy who had been over at the University of Washington. His football expertise was a little shaky.

We were throwing and catching before practice one day, when Jim Zorn overthrew one of the receivers. The ball slipped out of Jim's hand, giving Jack a chance to have a little fun.

"Harry, do you have the left-handed footballs out here?" he demanded.

Long pause. "Um, well, I thought I did." At which point Harry turned to his assistant. "Get the left-handed balls!"

Jack never told him there was no such thing.

A Decidedly Unfair Shake

Another one of Jack's rules forbade players from fraternizing with opponents on the field after games. There would be none of this going out to midfield and standing around chewing the fat, shaking hands, talking to guys you knew.

We were playing San Diego in a preseason game at the Kingdome and one of the Chargers' offensive tackles, Billy Shields, was a great friend of mine. We played together for three years at Georgia Tech.

The game was winding down and I was playing offense, so I was already at midfield. The gun sounded and I glanced over to the sidelines and I saw Billy Shields jogging out to say hello.

And here I was, backing away from him, waving my hand at him like the guy had some sort of awful, chronic disease. I managed to tell him to meet me outside the locker room.

He ran off and I hurried away into the locker room. But, alas, all Jack had to see was that one moment where Billy reached his hand out and we shook hands.

The next day, Jack calls everybody up after practice in Cheney.

"You know, men, we have rules on this team for a reason. And sometimes we have to reinforce those rules."

He called Jimmy Whitesel and Bruce Scott, the two trainers, and he told them to get about 300 yards away on one of the far practice fields, under the goal post. And then he told them to hold up this big cardboard sign reading "MY FRIEND" in big letters.

"Now, as you know, we like to get into the locker room after the games, but yesterday some of you decided that you wanted to see your friends anyway. Well, I want to reinforce this rule about getting off the field when the game is over."

He pulled out a little piece of paper.

"Will Peter Cronan, Terry Beeson and Steve Raible please come here?"

Not good.

"Now, we're going to practice how you should get off the field after the game. You three that decided to say hello to your friends on the Chargers yesterday, I want you to go sprint around those guys with the sign and then come back here."

And then he blew his whistle. The rest of the team was busting out laughing. They thought it was great. We sprinted all the way down there and we sprinted all the way back.

"Everybody got that idea? Any of you have any questions about that? Well, maybe there might be a few questions, so let's do that one more time."

He blew his whistle again. We went sprinting all the way down there, around MY FRIEND and all the way back. We did it three times. And we were just dragging by this time. And everybody was laughing.

To the outsider it seems like, well, what a nitpicky thing. But it got across his point... and it WAS very funny.

As a coach, you find a way to bring a team together. Whether it's to bring players together against the opponent or against the coach, I don't think Jack really cared. As long as we were together and believed in what we were doing and stuck together as a team.

Rules Are Rules

Jack Patera once cut a guy for refusing to shave a beard. "Look, we're an expansion team," Jack told him. "We've got to set a standard and I can't make exceptions. I know what you've done in the league, but if you want to play here, you've got to shave your beard because everybody else has."

The player, whose name escapes me, politely refused.

"All right," Jack said, "I'm going to let you go."

There was no animosity. Jack explained the rules and they agreed to disagree.

Giving Don Shula the Hard Sell

Nine minutes and change. That's how long poor Andre Hines needed to "run" around the practice fields at training camp in Cheney. Except no one could tell if out-of-shape Andre was running or walking. Suffice to say that the head man was not amused.

So 47-year-old Jack Patera commandeered the stopwatch from the trainer and walked around the track himself. Elapsed time: eight minutes. That's right, Jack Patera walked faster in 1980 than Hines ran as a rookie second-round pick from Stanford.

To be fair, Hines was a promising prospect in college. He was 275 pounds and had shown an ability to pull and cut people off. Jack always thought the guy might have done better had he signed as a free agent, without the pressure that comes with being a draft choice.

Whatever the case, trainers Bruce Scott and Jimmy Whitesel made it their life's work during camp to get this guy in shape. So in addition to the million other exercises they had Hines doing, Jimmy made him run up and down this hill adjacent to the practice fields. It wasn't very big as hills go, but make an offensive tackle run up it 25 times and his rear end is going to be dragging.

But it didn't matter. Andre kept gaining weight (he was having pizzas delivered to his dorm room, we later learned).

All these years later, Hines Hill still stands in tribute to Jack's penchant for conditioning. Andre wasn't so fortunate.

Jack shipped him to Miami that summer after a classic sell job that had Dolphins coach Don Shula scratching his head. Jack and Don played together with the old Baltimore Colts in 1955 and 1956, so they knew each other. But Don must have thought his old pal had gone mad.

"Well, Don, he's the worst player, the worst offensive lineman I've ever seen. We drafted him No. 2 and I don't know why. He's weak, he's not fast, he can't block anybody. But knowing you, you will probably make an All-Pro out of him."

Shula wasn't having it.

"Don't give me any of that bull, Jack."

"Don, I'm telling you, he's worthless."

"But he was a second-round draft choice."

"Yeah, but we made a mistake. This guy is awful."

Shula couldn't resist. He traded a conditional pick to Seattle for Hines, who lasted about two days in the Dolphins' camp.

"I couldn't believe what Jack was telling me," Shula recounted years later. "I figured that it had to be something personal, so I traded for him."

Jack the Hipper

Jacob Green is big on grooming. One time, at his golf tournament, Jack showed up wearing a hat with a pony tail on the back and "Silver Fox" written across the front.

It was pretty convincing, too. Someone even approached Jack after the round, wondering where the ponytail went.

Payback for the Writers

Jack took his share of heat in the local press, but he wasn't above exacting revenge in his own way.

They used to have him every so often as guest speaker at the weekly sportswriters' luncheon.

Well, Jack would go in after practice and then have a couple of drinks or something in his office and wait for deadline to pass before he actually came down and talked to the writers. And so they'd miss their deadlines.

He used to do things like that just for fun.

Two "Light" Practices

There was no such thing as minicamps in the old days. In fact, the only minicamp I ever attended as a player was the rookie orientation camp in April 1976, after the draft.

We had meetings and they fitted us for equipment and then we went out and had two practices. Basic stuff.

Well, years later, I read an old newspaper article that said we had two "light" practices.

What were they smoking? Jack had guys throwing up.

Grass Drills

Some guys called them up-downs. We knew them as grass drills.

You'd run in place until Jack barked out "front" or "back" and players dropped to the ground in the appropriate direction. You'd pop back up, run in place and wait for Jack to bark again.

We would stretch and all that stuff, then we'd do grass drills to start every practice. And I'll never forget Bob Newton, the guard we claimed off waivers from Chicago, just dying out there. He was so tired and he was probably hung over.

First of all, his knees were not even moving. Jack would say "front" and literally Bob would just throw himself down and land right on his face. Then it would take him like 30 seconds to get up off the ground and Jack would say "back" and you'd just see him fall flat on his back.

I mean, it was sad. He could kill you with those grass drills.

But that was the way we started every practice. Pretty soon, you got used to the grass drills and the gassers, just as you got used to a practice without water, even in Cheney.

And I remember only one guy not making it. Bill Olds, a fullback we got from the Colts, just hit the ground halfway through the seventh or eighth gasser on like the second day of camp in 1976. His legs just started to curl up on him.

And Jack just made it a point to say, "Look, I keep telling you, you have to hydrate before practice. I want you drinking all the fluids you can beforehand, and at night too, because that's the way it is. We're not out here long enough that we're going to do any damage to you."

Now, obviously, times have changed. Team trainers and doctors have all the water guys want at practice. But years ago, things were different. Somehow we all managed. We all survived.

A Method to Jack's Madness

We didn't have minicamps in the early years and besides, many players worked off-season jobs just to provide for their families.

Even the top picks weren't set for life. Steve Niehaus, the player we took first overall in the 1976 draft, never earned more than $90,000 in a season. It took me six years and a fistful of special teams bonuses to make that in a season.

So you had six preseason games, and players basically got themselves into shape in training camp.

And while Coach Patera was tough as hell on us, there was a method to his madness, and we could appreciate that.

The way Jack saw things, you didn't stay out on the practice field too long, because you ended up practicing your mistakes. You went out there, went intensely and went quick. Don't stand around, don't make mistakes, and get off the field. And get your conditioning in.

Jack always had time for his dogs. Still does.

Well, the 1981 season rolls around and we're struggling. We hit rock bottom with a 32-0 home loss to the Giants. The loss, our fifth straight, dropped us to 1-6 in the standings. Jack comes into the locker room afterward, and his 15-word postgame speech lingered ominously.

"Congratulations, you're now the worst team in the National Football League. I'll see you tomorrow."

The next day, we're at practice and Jack makes us run gassers, which we hadn't done since training camp, and we hit. We were out in full pads and we did all kinds of grass drills and then ran gassers afterwards and we were hitting in practice.

Keep in mind, we were 13 games into the season, counting preseason. Nowadays, most teams don't even practice until three days after a game, and hitting is kept to a minimum.

Well, guys were just falling out. I mean, guys who played on Sunday, their backs are tightening up every time they got in that three-point stance. And then came the gassers. People were just dying.

Jack thought we weren't in shape. He thought we were weak at the end of the game. Man, oh man, we paid for it.

And the next week we go to New York and beat the Jets back there, 19-3. Won three of our next four games, in fact.

You'd be hard pressed, though, to convince any of us at that moment that all that running and hitting was going to work.

Eternal Optimism

J ack Patera, in looking at that group of 125 prospects at that very first training camp, never thought he was up against anything. Quite the opposite, in fact.

"What an opportunity," Jack thought. "We're going to be the first expansion team to go 12-2."

They were 2-12 that first year, of course, but Jack honestly saw potential in that 1976 team.

"There's nothing but optimism in any coach's mind, no matter where he is," Jack said. "Whether he's an ex-Super Bowl champion or an expansion coach, he thinks, 'Boy, we've got a lot of work to do to see exactly who is going to be our team, but we've got so much talent that undoubtedly we'll filter it out, and it'll be fun coaching.'"

Jack had been part of the expansion process with the Cowboys. His general manager in Seattle, John Thompson, had gone through the formative years with the Vikings.

"People always told me how the best years of your life are going to be the first two or three years of an expansion team, because there's just an enthusiasm that is never going to be there again," Jack said. "And whether you win or not doesn't make any difference. Everybody's just excited. And I thought, 'Well, I agree with all of everything except whether we win or not. Because I'm sure we're going to win.'"

Winning Too Soon

Legendary Vikings coach Bud Grant, Jack's mentor in Minnesota, told him that the Seahawks won too quickly. Jack produced 9-7 records in our third and fourth seasons, a pretty remarkable feat.

But when the team slid backward in 1980 and 1981, the ground beneath Jack became a little less firm. Except he didn't know it at the time.

Tony Dorsett, Nearly a Hawk

Snapping up Curt Warner in the 1983 draft launched Seattle into the AFC championship game eight months later. But what if the fledgling Seahawks had drafted another running back, Tony Dorsett, instead of trading the second overall choice to Dallas in 1977?

The idea in trading down was to get more players. And in the end we got some guys who were good, but none of them close to the stature of a Tony Dorsett. When you think about what Dorsett could do as a running back, he would make everyone else around him better and he might have made a mediocre offensive line a lot better early on.

We didn't have a great line when Curt was a rookie, but he sure made that whole offense more effective. He made Steve Largent more effective as a receiver, because now we didn't have to depend on him all the time. It led to the moving out of Jim Zorn and the moving in of Dave Krieg, who was more in tune with the kind offense Chuck Knox wanted to run.

Steve August, Tom Lynch and Terry Beeson started a total of 205 games for us. Dorsett kept running all the way to Canton and the Pro Football Hall of Fame. Yet, as much as we could have used the Heisman Trophy-winning back from Pittsburgh, coach Jack Patera was looking to build depth.

"We went back and forth a lot on whether to take Dorsett or trade the second pick for more choices," Jack said. "But the kicker was that we wouldn't have made the trade had Tampa Bay taken Dorsett first overall. Because the Cowboys didn't want Ricky Bell, the running back from USC."

The Cowboys wanted Dorsett, and they got him when we sent the second pick to Dallas for the 14th pick and three second-rounders. We took a tackle (August), a guard (Lynch) and linebacker (Beeson). We also traded one of those second-round picks back to the Cowboys for receiver Duke Ferguson, who started eight games for us.

He Never Coached Again

The note left under Jack Patera's windshield wiper implored him to call the Lake Quinault Lodge—immediately. The 1982 players' strike was dragging on, and Jack had gone fishing. Fearing the worst upon discovering the note, Jack was initially relieved to learn of his firing after six-plus years as head coach.

"Who in the hell would get ahold of me with a truck parked in the woods on the river? They had to come about 16 miles and up the road another four or five, and at the time I thought, you know, there's something wrong with my family, or my child, or whatever."

The little old lady at the lodge, 80 years old and maybe five feet tall, broke the news over the phone. She wasn't the type to swear, but this time was different.

"Dammit, Jack, those bastards fired you!"

"What?"

"Yeah, you got a message down here to call (general manager) John Thompson. They fired you and John."

"Well, I'll be damned."

Jack's relief turned to anger, then disappointment. He wasn't even 50 years old, but he never coached again.

"The more I thought about it, the more disappointed I was that we didn't get a chance to finish what we started. You really devote your life to something. I just didn't want to get into that situation again where it's a one-way deal. So I thought it was time to get into my life's work."

Jack coached in an era when Pittsburgh, Dallas and Minnesota won with 10-year plans. He came to Seattle with similar aspirations.

"When I was hired, Lloyd Nordstrom was the managing general partner and it was the 10-year plan: We'll do it just like the Cowboys did it and the Pittsburghs and so forth. And then of course Lloyd died 17 days after I was hired."

The new managing general partner, Herman Sarkowsky, seemed to understand. The team finished 9-7 in 1978 and 1979, incredible success for an expansion franchise in those days. But when the record fell off over the next two years, Jack alluded to filling holes in the roster. That might have cost him.

"I had just signed a new contract. I thought things were going all right. I was very open and very honest about our team and what we had. But evidently Herman went in and reported this to the rest of the ownership group. And John Thompson was wondering what in the hell I told Herman. It was as though Herman thought we had nobody on the roster. I told John that I didn't tell him anything so bad. But evidently it made a big impression on John Nordstrom."

Jack was gone. Later, in retirement, he pondered the words former Baltimore Colts general manager Don Kellett spoke to him years before: "Let me tell you about coaching. It's the hardest way to make an easy living there is."

CHAPTER 7

Steve Largent

One of the most lopsided trades in NFL history brought a future Hall of Famer to Seattle in 1976 for an eighth-round draft choice. Steve Largent, himself only a fourth-round pick of the Houston Oilers a few months earlier, arrived a couple weeks before the regular season.

We played the last preseason game in Oakland, and Steve caught a couple touchdown passes. He ran routes like none of us had seen. I couldn't figure out how in the hell this guy could come in here able to run pass routes so well.

Part of the reason was because he knew the system. Jerry Rhome, our offensive coordinator, was at Tulsa when

Steve was there. So Steve knew the exact distance of the pass routes, exactly what Jerry wanted and how he wanted them run, and he had terrific body control, great quickness and, of course, the best hands I'd ever seen.

FIRST IMPRESSION:
Steve Largent

The original Seahawks headquarters teetered on the edge of Lake Washington, across the water from Seattle. Players leaving the locker room for the practice field encountered this beautiful expanse of green grass that led down to the water. It was a really gorgeous setting, like being on vacation every day.

And so Steve Largent walked out the door and onto the deck of the facility for the first time after we acquired him from the Oilers in August 1976. It was a couple days before our fifth preseason game and practice was ending. Here were Jim Zorn, Sam McCullum and me, along with former Eastern Washington standout Bob Picard and Ahmad Rashad, who was still in camp with us, just throwing passes after practice.

Largent regales in telling the story. He noticed me wearing No. 83, the number he had in college. He was hoping he would get that number back, but I already had it. So here he was looking up on that first day and he saw this No. 83 out there. I ran this quick slant, which we ran about six to seven yards toward the middle of the field. Well, I slipped on the grass and started to fall. The ball hit me in the head and bounced off my helmet.

At which point Largent turned and said, "I can play here." To this day, we always enjoy ribbing each other about it.

But it didn't take long for us to realize after Steve Largent walked in the building that day that he was far and away the best receiver we had.

Light Years Ahead of Everyone

The Seahawks, like most NFL teams, had rated Largent as a third- or fourth-round draft choice when he came out of Tulsa in 1976. So when Steve became available, Seattle made the trade.

Jerry Rhome was excited. But no one else knew what the organization was getting, including Jack Patera.

"He comes in and I had no more hope for him than a lot of people we had. But the first day he comes out there and turns around and looks the ball into his hands and he runs the right route … that was something we hadn't seen from a big-name player, Ahmad Rashad, in two months."

Steve Largent's battles with Lester Hayes were legendary.

It didn't take long to see that Steve was light years ahead of us in running routes. I never ran routes in college. We ran the wishbone at Georgia Tech, and it was block, block, block, go deep. Here was a guy with body control and the ability to lean, to get that defensive back right there, and then boom, he's over here. Lester Hayes said it best. He said covering Largent was like trying to cover smoke.

Largent almost never dropped a pass, even in practice. If your focus is that great all the time, then it becomes just like practice in the game. And that's the way it was for Steve. Jack Patera became a fan right away.

"The consistency of a player means more than the fact that he can make a great catch once in a while. Consistency is the No. 1 thing in life. How consistent are you? Do you catch a ball all the time or part of the time?"

Looking the Ball In

Receivers are told to keep their eyes on the ball until after the catch. We call it looking the ball in. Steve Largent took it one step further. He focused on the tip of the ball.

The tighter your focus, the thinking went, the more likely you were to block out everything else.

Tone It Down, Rook

Act like you've been there before. Steve Largent preached those words consistently. Brian Blades got the message loud and clear following one of the first catches of his NFL career. Here was this kid from the University of Miami, which had a reputation for flamboyance anyway, going through all these wild gyrations following some simple catch.

Brian jumped up off the ground and spun the ball like some dice or something and did this dance. He even gave the old first-down signal. And Largent came up behind him and grabbed him by the shoulder pads and literally threw him back to the huddle.

Basically, in no uncertain terms, Steve told him right then how a professional was supposed to act.

"You know, you just did your job by making that catch. You did absolutely nothing special. When you do something special, then you can celebrate. Act like you've been there before."

Steve Largent never drew attention to himself except by what he did on the field. Not by the extra-curricular stuff, but with his excellence. He was a teacher by example, and every so often by getting in people's faces and saying, "This is how you perform. This is what you're supposed to do on a regular basis."

I always thought that was a very telling thing about Steve and how he earned the respect of his teammates. Everybody said Dave Krieg was the leader of that offense, but Steve was the guy by virtue of his excellence and through his actions.

Brian Blades paid attention, too. I don't remember him doing much of that kind of celebrating after that. He was a clutch guy and a good team player. Brian became the kind of leader that Largent once was, helping to pass along some of those lessons.

Payback

The Seahawks swept the Broncos in 1988 for only the second time, helping them win their first AFC West title. All these years later, two memories linger from those games: Mike Harden's vicious cheap shot on Steve Largent in the season opener, and the payback that came so sweetly when the Broncos visited the Kingdome in December.

Steve had bounced up after big hits from guys like Jack Tatum. But the shot from Harden knocked him out for several minutes, mashing his facemask and knocking out two teeth. The league levied a $5,000 fine against Harden for the hit, but Largent extracted a heavier toll.

On December 11, 1988, Harden picked off a pass and headed upfield. Largent was waiting. Steve hit him so hard, the ball came loose and the Seahawks recovered. Seattle won the game, 42-14. Chuck Knox loved it.

"That was a great, great legal hit. Harden had hit him and really took advantage of Steve. And Steve was a lot tougher person, mentally and physically, than a lot of people gave him credit for."

Coach Largent

Chuck Knox's admiration for Steve Largent ran deep. When a broken elbow sidelined Steve for a time, Chuck turned him into another assistant coach.

"He would come out on the practice field before practice and he would have the scripted sheet of the plays we were going to run that day. He would get a ballboy and he would stand him over the ball and he would go out like

Steve Largent focuses on the task at hand prior to a big game against the Raiders at the L.A. Coliseum.

he's a wide receiver and he would jog through one of those patterns.

"And I thought so much of his input and everything that I had him prepare 'Largent's picks' for the game plan, the pass plays he liked the best against the defense that we were going to see. He had looked at the film. I kept him involved all the way. We'd be in a meeting and I'd say, 'Well, Steve likes this.' Some players like everything, especially if the ball's going to go to them. This guy gave everything some thought. I had so much respect for him.

"I still hear from him. He calls me every now and then. He called me when he was in the House of Representatives.

He'd bring up some story. He just is a wonderful, wonderful person. Very bright and hard working."

Boys Will Be Boys

Steve Largent's favorite prank was the old shaving-cream-in-the-receiver gag. He would lather up the telephone, place the receiver back on the hook and lay the trap.

"Raibs, phone's for you."

Who looks at the receiver before he answers? You'd just jam that shaving cream right in your ear. And Steve would laugh like a little kid. Nobody was safe, either, as Jack Patera recalled years later.

"They did that at my house one time when the offense was there. That wasn't the first time that I'd ever heard of that. I didn't think it was funny or unfunny. I just thought, 'Jesus Christ, these guys are 24 years old.'"

But we were still kids, and none more so than Largent.

Family's the Thing

As a youngster growing up in Oklahoma, Steve Largent had little to be secure about. His father left home when Steve was six. His mother remarried ... to an alcoholic. Young Steve cried himself to sleep and vowed life would never be like this when he married and had a family. Steve and Terry have been married for three decades and have four children. But that, like the rest of Steve Largent's life, has not been without its challenges. I remember Steve telling me once that the birth of his son, Kramer, with spina bifida, was far from a tragedy.

"It was a blessing to Terry and I. We've always said if we were to do it over again, we wouldn't change a thing for us or Kramer. For Kramer, we'd wish him complete 100 percent health, as every parent would. There is nothing harder than to stand helpless beside the bed of your son or daughter who is in the hospital knowing that it doesn't matter how much money you have, how powerful you are, how popular you are. You can't do anything. You'd trade places with them in a second, but you can't do it."

Steve and Terry have learned plenty about life and themselves through their walk with Kramer.

"We learned that God is in control and we're not. We're very independent people. We think we can do just about anything and we've found out there's a whole lot of things we don't have control over. Literally we're helpless. So I think at a moment like this, and we've had others, where your faith and your life is in crisis, that it's the foundation you have in your life— your family, your loved ones, your faith—that you find out how secure you are in those things."

Proving the Skeptics Wrong

In 1976, Steve Largent joined the fledgling Seahawks and beat long odds to become one of the best players of his generation. He retired with more catches (819) than anyone in league history. Through 14 seasons and seven Pro Bowls, Largent proved the skeptics wrong.

"Nothing has come easy for me. I've always been an overachiever: too small, too slow. 'Can't do that' is actually something I recognize fueled my jet engines."

Why beat one DB when you can beat two? Nobody stopped Steve Largent.

A Career Complete

When it all ended on a December Sunday in 1989, the toughest player the franchise ever knew showed he was only human in acknowledging his teammates and his fans. With tears streaming down his face, Steve Largent struggled to get the words out.

"All I can say is thank you from my family and God bless. Have a Merry Christmas. I thank you."

It wasn't terribly loquacious for a future politician, but it was right on the money.

"I wish I could have had time to say it was a pleasure playing with them and thank them for their help and making me what I've become and be able to really appreciate and thank those people that I feel like I stood on their shoulders," Steve said later. "They lifted me to the heights that I obtained."

Canton Bound, With Class

Relatively few people outside the organization are privileged to know Gary Wright. Here is all one needs to know about the Seahawks' vice president of communications: Steve Largent selected Gary to be his presenter at the Pro Football Hall of Fame.

The choice tells you plenty about Largent, too. It was a wonderful gesture and one that I don't think anybody would have thought of except for Steve. It just made so much sense. Here was a guy in Gary who had been there from Day One, having hired on as director of publicity in 1976. Everybody liked and respected him, as they do to this day.

Had Steve chosen a player, other teammates might have felt left out. Choosing Gary made everyone feel good. Steve approached him about six months before his election to Canton.

"I'm not trying to jinx anything and I'm not counting on anything before it happens," Steve told him, "but if I go in, I've decided who I want to be my presenter."

Numerous candidates flashed through Gary's mind, from Zorn to Krieg and beyond. Steve's choice sent Gary reeling.

"I about fell off my chair. It's just a fabulous honor. I was absolutely speechless and then tried to talk him out of it."

Steve's mind was made up. On July 29, 1995, Gary Wright rewarded the greatest player in Seahawks history with three minutes of carefully crafted eloquence. As Gary retreated from the podium, Largent hugged him and said, "I knew you were the right guy."

A Jersey for Pete's Sake

When Steve Largent set the NFL record with his 100th touchdown catch, everyone assumed his No. 80 jersey would head directly to the Pro Football Hall of Fame. Steve had other ideas. In a move that caught everyone by surprise but made perfect sense upon reflection, he handed the jersey to our beloved play-by-play man, Pete Gross.

Cancer had claimed Pete's kidney earlier that season. And so when Steve set the record with a leaping catch in Cincinnati on December 12, 1989, his jersey had Pete's name written all over it.

Steve Largent surprised everyone, including Pete Gross, after setting an NFL record with his 100th touchdown catch.

If Steve had thought about it beforehand, he did a marvelous job of not saying anything about it and then just doing it. And he expected nothing in return. I think that's part of what makes Steve so great. He does what he thinks is right as opposed to what would get him the most mileage. As a politician, maybe he thought of things differently. But I think it's just part of his makeup. That's just the way he is.

Two Strikes and Largent Was Out

Crossing the picket lines during the player strikes of 1982 and 1987 came at a personal cost to Largent. Those were awful times for everyone involved, and Steve was no exception. He broke down and cried in front of the team during an impassioned speech he gave at Showy's bar in Cheney before the '82 strike. Steve was explaining why he planned to cross the line, and it wasn't easy.

That was my first season working for KIRO-TV sports. The station sent me to some auditorium in Bellevue to cover the Seahawks' strike vote. After a while, the doors came flying open, and I soon realized how much things had changed for me personally.

"You're against us, too, huh, Raibs?" a former teammate said upon seeing me with camera crew in tow. "We thought you were our friend."

"I'm just covering the story. You had an announcement to make, for crying out loud."

Largent, Jim Zorn and Dan Doornink were the most prominent players to cross the lines in '82.

When the second strike rolled around five years later, Largent was willing to show solidarity, but only to a point.

"I'm willing to walk to support you guys and it's costing me $50,000 a game. But I don't care about money as long as the team stays together. That's more important to me."

Well, Steve eventually crossed, and when he did, he hooked up with Jeff Kemp to set the team record with 15 catches in a game. He nearly had my entire fifth season in that one game against the Lions.

Steve set the record, but nobody won in those strikes. Bitterness and animosity prevailed. Kenny Easley was a union rep and he wouldn't even speak to Largent. Steve owned Seattle in those days, but the hard feelings from that second strike played a role in his decision to move back to Oklahoma upon his retirement.

Fifteen Catches and an Asterisk

Largent set the franchise record with 15 catches in a strike game against the Lions. He might have caught 40 balls that day had he not taken himself out of the game.

"You had a Hall of Famer running pass routes on bus drivers and mailmen from Detroit," former team vice president Randy Mueller said. "It was comical watching these guys try to cover him. It was embarrassing, but it was funny."

Asked why they didn't resort to double-coverage, Lions coach Darryl Rogers served up a classic quote: "Why embarrass two players when you can just embarrass one?"

Steve Largent runs out of the Kingdome tunnel for the last time.

Presidential Sendoff

Two U.S. presidents taped congratulatory videos saluting Steve when he retired. But former NFL commissioner Pete Rozelle probably put it best when he said, "It took only seven months to find my successor, but it will be years before anyone with the character, human decency and on-the-field skills will be found to replace Steve Largent."

We're still looking.

Down, but Not Out

For all the defensive backs that Steve Largent beat over his football career, the only opponent he couldn't overcome was, of all things, cockfighting. When Steve ran for the Oklahoma governorship as a former four-term U.S. congressman, he was the hands-down favorite. But in the closing days of the campaign he lost his lead and ultimately the race.

An initiative to ban cockfighting in Oklahoma brought out more Democrats than the state had seen in years, swinging the election in favor of Steve's opponent. It was as bitter as any defeat Steve suffered on the football field, and lasted longer.

"I have suffered many setbacks in my life and this was one of the most painful and public setbacks that I ever experienced. Totally unanticipated. I never considered losing.

"It was painful, it hurt a lot, but I will tell you that one of the things about me is that I'm very resilient and I bounce back. Maybe it's because I was an athlete. Maybe it's because I've had a lot of hard knocks in my life. But the real measure of a man is how long it takes him to get back up. And it doesn't take me very long."

CHAPTER 8

Kenny Easley

O ff-season minicamps didn't exist when we landed a big-hitting safety in the first round of the 1981 draft. That meant training camp was the first time we ever saw Kenny Easley.

Rookies reported to camp early, so the veterans arrived just about the time the young guys' legs were turning to rubber. Which was perfect, because they'd be so damn tired and they'd be wondering why they even decided to try to play pro football. That was the whole idea. You tried to make those guys feel as bad as you could.

So we're watching them practice and they're playing against other rookies, so they're all pretty equal out there—except for Easley. You can tell he has some ability out there, this long-legged kid in the secondary. He looks taller than he really is, but it's because of his lean, muscular build. He's got this great flowing running motion and high knees. So we say, "Well, we'll find out, rook, what you're made of here come tomorrow."

We veterans go get our physicals and show up for that morning practice and we're out there running seven-on-seven passing drills. I run a shallow drag route and Largent runs a crossing route.

And the idea is for the backside receiver to run a post. So here comes Easley from his safety spot and he bites on the crossing route, and there goes the backside receiver on the deep post. Easley took about three steps toward that crossing route and then figured out what was going on. Anyone else would have been toast, but Easley turned, broke on the ball and got there in time to intercept the pass.

Kenny Easley dominated like few safeties in NFL history.

We all just looked at each other as if to say, "Holy crap, this guy can play. He is really something now. He's the real deal."

Easley's Hawaiian Non-Vacation

Lockers at the Pro Bowl were assigned by jersey number. That placed Kenny Easley (No. 45) next to Raiders tight end Todd Christensen (No. 46) one year in the 1980s.

Easley went to the game as a safety, but coaches moved him to cornerback because Mike Haynes was hurt. Well, Easley allowed not a single completed pass for the entire second quarter against an NFC receiving corps featuring Art Monk, James Lofton and Roy Green.

"To see this guy go from being that six-foot-three, 205-pound monster in the middle, then put the glove on somebody out on the corner, I said this is unbelievable," Christensen recounted. "Remember, this is a Pro Bowl. It's not like guys are saying, 'Oh, yes, I'm going to kill myself for 10 grand.' You can actually smell the Mai Tais in the huddle."

Knowing Easley, he probably smelled blood. Christensen was still in awe when the players reconvened at their lockers during halftime.

"Kenny turns to me and he actually grumbles and says, 'You know what? I would have done a lot better if I'd had smaller shoulder pads, but I have to wear these big ones,'" Christensen said. "And I couldn't believe it. The guy was a stud. I was just so impressed."

Christensen put Easley up there with some of the all-time greats, including Hall of Famer Ronnie Lott.

"It goes without saying what Ronnie did in his career," Todd said. "But in all candor—and this is no knock on Ronnie—Kenny Easley was a better football player."

Pure Domination

Mark Clayton and Mark Duper enjoyed great careers as Dan Marino's primary targets with Miami, but they weren't stupid. The Marks Brothers, as they were known, seemed particularly aware of Kenny Easley. They certainly felt his presence during Seattle's big playoff win over the Dolphins after the '83 season.

"You're not supposed to be able to dominate a game from safety, but Easley did," former Seahawks executive Randy Mueller said. "Ask the Marks Brothers about him. They wanted no part of Kenny Easley, and really, that's why we were able to beat them and be so effective.

"He just whacked the snot out of those guys, whether they were going to catch it or not. They came across the middle and he would level them. He was awesome. You forget he's 6-3, 215 pounds. That's a big human being. And he had the look, too. He had the look of a killer."

Mueller knew the look all too well. As a ballboy back in the days when Jack Patera wouldn't let players drink during two-a-days, Mueller found himself smuggling ice to a certain bad-ass safety. In fact, Easley made sure Randy supplied the entire secondary.

"I'd have towels in my ball-bag wrapped up with the ice in the middle and I would stand behind the line of scrimmage with my hands behind my back full of ice and they would come by and take ice out of my hands. I was scared to death that Jack was going to find out. I made $44 a week as a ballboy. I made three times that sneaking ice out on the field. And Easley was the ringleader. He'd look at me and he would be so pissed if I didn't have ice. I was deathly afraid of Jack, but I was more afraid of Easley and the rest of them."

An Aggressive Type of Game

Kenny Easley pushed the words through that sinister half-smile of his and launched them directly into NFL Films immortality.

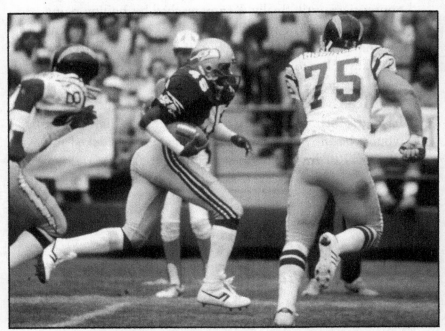

Kenny Easley once picked off three passes in a game vs. San Diego.

"I'm vicious, there's no doubt about it. I play the game in a vicious manner. I don't go out there to hurt anyone, but my game is an aggressive type of game."

Ready to Rumble

Each first-round pick looked after the next back in the early days. And so Jacob Green, our top choice in 1980, was supposed to make sure Kenny Easley became properly initiated in NFL life. The hazing wasn't too bad, but every rookie had to sing in the dining hall, and big Jake wasn't about to let Kenny off the hook. Not only did Easley sing, but he did whatever else Jacob thought appropriate until, finally, Kenny reached his boiling point.

"I don't know what I did," Easley told his girlfriend on the phone one night, "but if that Jacob Green so much as talks to me tomorrow, even says one word to me, we're going to fight."

Jacob was oblivious, of course, but as luck would have it, their paths didn't cross the next day. There would be no fight. But Jacob generally picked on Easley all of his rookie season and especially in training camp.

Once a Teammate, Always a Teammate

Kenny Easley is a tough, intense guy. But when I saw him a few years ago for the first time in at least a decade, it was amazing how we just sort of picked up where we left off.

He and Jacob Green were down in Arizona playing in a charity golf tournament. Dave Krieg and I also happened to be in the area, so Dave called and asked if I wanted to join the three of them for a beer.

I see Jacob at fundraising events and I keep in touch with Dave, but I hadn't seen "Ease" in at least 10 years. And while, yes, he looked a little older and the hair was a little grayer, he still looked fit considering the kidney transplant and everything else he had been through. And it was almost as though we hadn't missed a beat.

I think that's one of the great things about being teammates at one time in your life. No matter how far away you get from the game, you walk back in the same room with these guys that you cried and bled and fought and played the game with, and it's amazing. You can just pick right back up again.

The four of us talked all evening over loud music coming out of a jukebox, and it seemed like 1981 all over again.

CHAPTER 9

The Man from Milton

D ave Krieg was lucky to be a Seahawk and he knew it. One of the team's personnel men owed a favor to Rudy Gaddini, Dave's old coach back at Milton College. And so Dick Mansberger, then player-personnel director under GM John Thompson, was pushing to sign this wide-eyed free agent quarterback from this anonymous school in Milton, Wisconsin.

As a rookie in 1980, Dave showed up for his first pre-season game not knowing what to expect. The Kingdome was maybe half full for warm ups and Dave was basically just enjoying his first taste of NFL life. He figured he'd just grab as many sets of wristbands as he could to take back to Wisconsin after he got cut.

Before long, the team went back into the locker room for a final word from Jack Patera. Much to Dave's surprise, the Kingdome was packed and rocking by the time the Seahawks ran back onto the field for the opening kickoff. It was an unbelievable feeling for a guy whose first airplane ride had been the one he took to Seattle for minicamps.

"I remember it like it was yesterday. First of all, I was hyperventilating because I was so nervous just being in the Kingdome in a professional uniform. Then it dawned on me ... all these people in one place with a roof and walls, and I'm claustrophobic."

So Dave was hyperventilating and claustrophobic before his first preseason game as a professional football player.

Nearly two decades later, David Michael Krieg retired from the game holding down the No. 8 spot on the NFL's all-time passing yardage list. Oh, and another thing: The top seven were guys named Marino, Elway, Moon, Tarkenton, Fouts, Montana and Unitas.

Thrilled to Be in the League

Dave Krieg (Milton College) and Ron Essink (Grand Valley State) didn't exactly play their college ball at USC or Michigan. They seemed thrilled to be in the league instead of some paper mill. So when a coach from Simon Fraser University asked the three of us to help with a football clinic up in Canada, Krieg and Essink were all for it.

This was the summer of '81, a year after they were drafted. I was a five-year vet. But Krieg, in particular, was about as green as grass.

Dave Krieg, right, could always count on Paul Skansi.

We got up there and the coach put us up in a nice hotel. It was a Saturday night, so we asked someone in the lobby where we might grab a quick beer. The locals were helpful.

"Go out the front door, turn right around the corner and there's a bar right there."

So we walked in and sat down. It was dark, I wasn't paying much attention and my back was to the main part of the room, anyway. We were drinking beer and the music started up real loud.

Dave and Ron were sitting across from me and pretty soon their eyes got bigger than saucers. As luck would have it, we'd walked into a strip club without knowing it. Honest. The stage, complete with obligatory brass pole, was directly behind me. I never saw it. Dave and Ron just about fainted.

We worked the clinic that weekend and had a good time up there. Right about then, I think Dave and Ron really liked the whole idea of being in pro football.

Seventh String

Dave Krieg was the seventh-string quarterback when he started out at Milton. The same fate awaited him in the NFL. And despite a strong showing in training camp, Dave made the final roster only after Steve Myer suffered a career-ending back injury in practice.

Even then, the talk among veterans was about signing an experienced passer to serve alongside Jim Zorn and Sam

Dave who? Jim Zorn, Sam Adkins and Steve Myer weren't too worried about the undrafted kid from Milton College.

Adkins. Dave didn't say anything to us at the time, but that kind of talk irked him.

"What do you mean, go out and get somebody? You've got me. I can play. I can help this team win."

Of course, Dave always remembers the stuff that hurt. The digs and slights motivated him. No one ever thought he could do the job, even after he'd been doing it for years. Dave was playing in Pro Bowls not long before the Seahawks were dreaming about guys like Kelly Stouffer and even Dan McGwire.

And so Dave's whole reason for being in life was to prove those doubters wrong. He always remembered that day when Steve Myer got hurt and nobody thought Dave was the answer. He was the answer, of course, only not right away.

Be Prepared

We lost our final nine games in 1980 and Dave Krieg figured there was no way he would play in the season finale. But then Jim Zorn went down to injury and Sam Adkins ate his mustache in that horrific collision with Broncos linebacker Tom Jackson.

Dave was suddenly the guy, if only briefly.

The first play Dave ran was called 90 Hot B-Option. Ninety referred to the protection scheme with the running backs releasing on little under routes. If the blitz was coming and it's a hot route, the "B" option allowed the quarterback to throw a quick pass into the flat.

Problem was, Dave didn't know any of this. So he got to the line of scrimmage, surveyed the scene and thought something like, "Oh, man, look ... these are the Denver Broncos!" The center snapped the ball and

Dave had no idea where to go with the ball. Ninety Hot B-Option meant nothing to him at that moment. The Broncos drilled him on the spot.

That's when Dave realized he needed to study if he ever hoped to succeed in the bigs.

Tears in Cincinnati

The kid from Milton was no match for the tests offensive coordinator Jerry Rhome gave to keep his players sharp. Dave Krieg's scores read like a golfer's nine-hole nightmare: 52, 58, 56. Finally, after weeks of frustration, there was progress.

Dave scored a 74 heading into the 1981 opener at Cincinnati. His thoughts were turning positive. "I'm ready to compete for a place in the lineup on this ball club." And then there was the test Jerry returned to Dave at the hotel in Cincinnati. The words written across the top cut Dave to the core: "THERE IS NO WAY I CAN PLAY YOU IN THIS GAME WITH YOUR LACK OF KNOWLEDGE OF OUR OFFENSE."

Dave walked out of the meeting room and into the lobby with tears in his eyes. He was crushed. There in the lobby were his parents, who had driven all the way from Wisconsin to see their kid on the field in a National Football League game. And here Dave's coach had just told him he might never play.

Dave Krieg, future Pro Bowl passer and team leader, went up to his room and cried.

Bouncing Back

Dave Krieg was starting by the end of that 1981 season. Jim Zorn took over for parts of the next two years as Jack Patera gave way to interim coach Mike McCormack and then Chuck Knox.

Dave gave fans a glimpse of the future in the final game of the strike-shortened 1982 season. His 19-yard touchdown pass to Roger Carr with 47 seconds left was the difference against Denver that day. Krieg led the offense 87 yards in 10 plays, with no time-outs—a nice comeback from the dreary days of "90 Hot B-Option" and the excoriation from Jerry Rhome back in Cincinnati.

Winning Time

The franchise was still looking for its first playoff berth when Chuck Knox made the change. Seattle was 4-4 and trailing Pittsburgh by a 27-0 count during that 1983 season. Dave Krieg made the Steelers sweat before that game was over, and the rest of the league took notice by season's end.

Dave led the Seahawks to the AFC title game that year. Playoff appearances followed in 1984, 1987 and 1988.

The 1986 team might have been more dangerous than any of them, but a 10-6 record wasn't enough to get the Seahawks into the playoffs that season. Nobody wanted to play them. They beat Dallas on Thanksgiving day by a 31-14 count. They pinned a 37-0 loss on the Raiders in a December game on *Monday Night Football*, the Raiders' worst defeat since 1962. They beat Denver, 41-16, and won at San Diego, 34-24.

People razz Dave for all the fumbles, but he was 70-49 (.588) as the starter in Seattle. The team responded to his leadership. Dave loved the game and never took it for granted. Some of us dismissed rookies as guys we'd send home after training camp. Not Dave.

"I always looked at other quarterbacks they brought in, even when I was starting. Any of these guys can beat me out if I don't work hard. I was one of those guys. I had to work hard just to get that opportunity to one day become the starting quarterback. I never took that for granted. Ever."

Whatever You Do, Don't Think

The most memorable play in Dave Krieg's career, at least in the regular season, was that last-second touchdown pass to Paul Skansi at Arrowhead Stadium on November 11, 1990. The Seahawks hadn't won there in a decade, and Dave had no business even being on the field for the play that defines his toughness, resolve and overall resourcefulness.

That was the notorious Derrick Thomas seven-sack game. Early on, Dave audibled to a pass play, dropped back and never even got his head around to look to the back side. Derrick Thomas just drilled him. Dave's facemask was the first thing that hit the ground. Dave knew then it was going to be a long day. Thomas was just insane in those days, and that Kansas City crowd could make your ears bleed.

Dave came off the field, half-blinded by this shot from Derrick Thomas. He couldn't see, he couldn't think,

Chuck Knox leads the cheers during a raucous celebration in the locker room at Arrowhead Stadium on November 11, 1990.

and his brains were jangled. Then came the hard part: answering to the head coach. "Well, I audibled," Dave managed. "I thought they were going to blitz."

Chuck just about bit his head off. "LISTEN, DON'T YOU THINK! EVERY TIME YOU THINK, YOU HURT THIS TEAM! Just run the play I send in."

The rest of the day followed a familiar script. Derrick Thomas coming off the corner. Derrick Thomas drilling Dave in the back. Derrick Thomas flushing Dave out of the pocket. Somehow they managed to stay in the game. It came down to the last play and "90 All Go" was the call: four receivers, everybody go down field, see if Dave can find someone before he gets killed. He found Derrick Thomas right away. In his face, grabbing him around the waist.

"All I remember was I kind of just whipped around," Dave said.

Thomas spun around like a kid flying off a carousel. Dave saw Paul Skansi between the safety and the cornerback in that one window where Dave could throw the ball. Dave let it fly. Someone hit him in the chin right about then, so Dave never saw where the ball went.

"All I knew was there was this insane amount of noise and I let the ball go and it got very quiet," Dave said. "I never doubted what happened. I knew we had a touchdown."

Laying It on the Line

Some quarterbacks celebrate touchdowns by running downfield and piling onto their receivers. Dave Krieg usually sought out his linemen first. He knew those guys made it happen. Besides, he could always catch up with his receiver on the sideline.

His line loved him for that. Not that Dave couldn't be intense. One time in pregame warmups, Dave ripped into his teammates when some of them broke the huddle a little early. Guys tend to get lazy and start filtering out of the huddle after hearing the part of the play that pertains to their specific position.

"Nobody leaves the huddle until I break the huddle!" Dave screamed.

Edwin "Pearl" Bailey, our big guard, jumped in Dave's face. "Shut up and call the play!"

They were going back and forth in pregame warmups and the whole team was looking at them like they were crazy. They went back into the locker room and Pearl came over and slapped Dave on the butt. "Come on, Mudbone, let's go out there and win a football game."

Dave's point resonated. He was running the show and no one was going to leave his huddle until Dave was finished. That's the way you want your quarterback to think. And Dave sure did.

Pro Bowl Bound

Making his first Pro Bowl appearance after the 1984 season was a highlight for Dave Krieg. Here was a guy from Milton who played on a field that was basically dirt down the middle and cornfields on both sides, with a rusty goalpost at the end.

The Dave Krieg story is almost better than the Jim Zorn story. At least Jim went to training camp with the Cowboys and people knew who he was. Dave was just a shot out of the blue. Maybe that's one reason he never really got his due.

CHAPTER 10

Planes, Trains and Automobiles

These are business trips, men, not weekend getaways. Every coach, at one time or another, has drilled that point home to his players. And I suppose it applies to the rest of us, too. And sometimes not.

For every hassle-free trip into enemy territory, there's a reminder that even the best-laid plans can go awry.

Perfectly Suited

Jack Patera's dress code for road trips impacted some guys more than others. Dave Krieg actually had to stop at JC Penney's to buy a tie and sport coat on his way to the airport for his first road trip.

Sensing something had gone awry with the tie, Krieg went to adjust it on the plane and, as luck would have it, the tie came loose. It was a clip-on. Steve Largent, a practical joker whose cruelty knew few bounds, grabbed the tie and took off running around the plane with it.

Poor Dave.

Bring in the Jaws of Life

Pete and Wayne were regulars at Anthony's Star of the Sea Restaurant in San Diego long before I joined the broadcast team in 1982. The tradition continued for years.

Pete always ordered the abalone. Wayne and I split the sole admiral, which was almost the whole fish split in half, stuffed with shrimp and crab meat and spices, then broiled to perfection. There wasn't a better meal in San Diego, or anywhere for that matter.

And Wayne always used to talk about the pumpernickel crisps. He loved those things. Wayne never met, I don't think, a food group he didn't like, quite frankly. He wasn't crazy about vegetables, but he ate them.

So this was the favorite haunt. And whatever it would take to get to Anthony's Star of the Sea, or to get food from there, Wayne would do.

We were playing the Rams in Anaheim one year. We got to the hotel when Pete and Wayne told me they had reservations—at Anthony's.

"But we're in Los Angeles, for God sakes," I tell them.

"Road trip," they say.

So here we go. The three of us drive down to San Diego and have, yet again, an exquisite meal. And of course Wayne had 37 helpings of other people's meals and other dishes. The bananas foster was incredible.

On the drive back, Wayne lies down in the back seat. The guy could sleep anywhere.

So we're driving along, and with God as my judge, this actually happened. We're doing 70 or 75, and this van literally slides right into my lane. So I bang the brakes. And I thought we got hit from behind. The whole front seat moved. The force threw Pete and me forward.

And I grabbed the wheel, I hung onto the wheel.

"Holy smokes, Peter, what happened? We just got hit."

And almost at the same time, Pete and I both looked back and Wayne had rolled off the back seat. And because he was on his side, he had rolled and fallen between the back and front seats, face first. The floor is right up next to his nose and his stomach is sort of on the hump and he's pinned in between the seats.

And he starts groaning. "You S.O.B., you did that on purpose."

"Wayne, I swear, I did not do it on purpose."

So I slow down and pull over into the far right-hand lane because we have to move the seat as far forward as it would go to relieve the pressure and let Wayne fall down to the floorboards. And now it takes him a while to get up.

I'm reaching around the back, Pete is reaching over the seat, we're trying to grab ahold of his shirt and his coat and pull him up and we finally sit him up.

Pete and I laughed about that for years afterward. "Remember the time Wayne did the turtle thing and got pinned?"

Wayne always thought we did it on purpose.

What State Are We In?

After one broadcast in Kansas City, our intrepid sideline reporter Wayne Cody decided he knew a better route from Arrowhead Stadium to the airport.

"Raibs, you drive and I'll direct, and we'll go over surface country roads and get to the airport," Wayne said.

And of course we got lost. I'm telling you, I think we crossed the border into Kansas without even knowing it. We saw everything but Dorothy and the house falling out of the sky. We were out there forever, and finally, just by the grace of God and only because I had young eyes, I picked up the speck of an airplane in the distance.

So we decided to drive in that direction. And we just kept driving. The whole time Peter doesn't say a thing. He's in the back seat with Norm Graham and he is just livid. I've never see Pete Gross angry, but he got this little half-smile on his face like, we're screwed, we're going to miss the plane, and we've never missed a charter flight.

This was the one time I wish he had had shrimp scampi in the car, because I was afraid we were going to die with nothing to eat but some corn out in these fields.

And so we are flying. I'm doing 85 miles an hour in this Lincoln Town Car, pulling into the airport. I pull up in front of the gate where I know the plane is, throw it in park, and I have two wheels up on the sidewalk. As we're running with our gear, I tossed the keys and a $20 bill to the guy at the gate and pleaded with him to take the car back to Hertz.

They were just closing the door to the plane. And of course we had just lost the game—we never won in Kansas City—and Coach Knox was in no mood to wait for Moe, Larry and Curly.

"That's it, we're going," he finally grumbled, but someone talked him into waiting another minute.

And of course the coaches sat up front, so we had to walk past them to get to our seats. And my God, the stares we got. Sweat was pouring off of us and I felt like a player again, like I was going to have to run laps in the plane on the way home.

All because of Wayne.

Drinks on Chuck

There were other times—well, one time, actually—when we didn't want to leave Kansas City. Dave Krieg's game-winning touchdown pass to Paul Skansi will forever live in Seahawks lore. The date was November 11, 1990 and Dave's 25-yard strike on the final play of the game handed Seattle its first win at Kansas City's Arrowhead Stadium since 1980.

"We got in our shotgun formation there, hit a little screen pass to John L. Williams, he takes it inside the 30-yard line," Chuck Knox recalled. "Now we've got time for one play, and the crowd noise is unbelievable. My left tackle is going against Derrick Thomas and Derrick went by him just like that. David Krieg spun around, threw the ball and hit Paul Skansi to tie the game, 20-20."

Note that Chuck didn't take the PAT for granted even all these years later. Once a coach, always a
coach.

That was the day Derrick Thomas set the NFL
record with seven sacks in a game. Derrick didn't get
to Dave on the play that mattered most, but Dave was
obviously hurting afterward. In fact, he was so long in
the locker room after the game that he missed the bus
to the airport. So we gave him a ride in our rental car.

Turns out there were mechanical problems with
the plane and nowhere to go but the watering hole
that happened to be adjacent to our gate. So I turned
to Dave and told him I owed him a beer for the touchdown pass that finally got us a win in Kansas City.

Well, pretty soon here comes Chuck Knox and
Reggie McKenzie and half the plane. We took over the
place and bought every ounce of alcohol in that bar,
except for the Mr. Clean under the sink. And I think
Reggie might have had some of that.

When it was all over, Chuck dropped his credit
card and said, "Here, take care of my boys."

I can't remember where we stayed that year, but we
stayed at the same hotel the next season because Chuck
would do anything to break our unlucky streak in Kansas
City.

Airport Security? What's That?

We were supposed to go in a back gate at Boston's
Logan Field one time but we couldn't find the gate.
And the traffic was just abominable, the worst. We were
again running late, but finally we could see the plane. We
found a gate.

There was this kind of a security shack and we could see the plane, but we couldn't get through the gate. And we couldn't get their attention. We're honking the horn, we're standing at the fence screaming and yelling. Nobody can hear us over the roar of these jet engines.

Finally, some airport guy in an old pickup truck comes driving up. We tell him we're supposed to be on the Seahawks charter. We start showing him media guides and radio gear, and he agrees to help.

"Jump in."

"Jump in what?"

"Jump in the truck."

So Pete and Wayne sat in the seat up in the cab. Problem was, there was no cushion on their part of the seat. It was literally just springs. So Peter is pulling a spring out of his hind end all the way across this runway, and Wayne is like halfway down to the floorboard.

Norm and I are sitting on the tailgate with our feet dangling off, and we're driving across the tarmac.

Here are four nimrods riding across a runway in a pickup truck with Jethro Bodine at the wheel. We get to the plane, and it was a six-hour trip from Boston back to Seattle on those old Alaska flights.

Our rental car was probably on blocks minutes after we parked it. But we called Hertz anyway and told them where to find the car.

"Yeah, that car, there's a security gate about three miles back behind the airport and you'll find it back there somewhere."

"Well, you're not supposed to leave it there, Mr. Cody."

"Well, I know, but we were late, and blah blah blah."

God knows if any of those cars ever got back. If they got back at all, they stunk from shrimp of some kind or some sort of pumpernickel crisp inside or they just found them with no tires and no seats inside, somewhere behind an airport.

Family Atmosphere (No Ifs, Ands or Duck)

The Nordstrom family instilled a family atmosphere that never entirely went away. Their original team plane, Seahawks 1, was an Alaska Airlines 727 featuring brass nameplates above the seats and murals emblazoned with the work of team photographer Corky Trewin.

Elmer Nordstrom, shaking hands with cornerback Dave Brown, believed in creating a family atmosphere.

Elmer and Kitty Nordstrom would pass out Christmas presents on the plane if we happened to be traveling during the holidays. The respect for them was palpable, like they were the parents of this giant football family.

Behind the scenes, our Alaska Airlines rep was scrambling to make things comfortable. Jeff Pinneo had a tough job. He was in his early 20s at the time, trying to put out potential fires before the smoke reached Jack Patera or Chuck Knox.

One time there were concerns that the menu, featuring duck, might be a problem. Word filtered back to Jeff that some considered the choice too exotic. But when Jeff approached the head coach, Jack told him to "just tell 'em it's chicken."

Jeff complied and dinner was served. A short time later, one of the flight attendants approached Jeff with a message. Steve Largent wanted to see him. Something about the menu.

"Jeff, I understand this is chicken?"

"Yes, it is."

Silence.

"Jeff, this is not chicken."

Pinneo could feel himself turning red. He'd been caught between the head coach and the star receiver. There was only one way out.

"You're right, Steve, it's not chicken."

"So you lied?"

Jeff didn't know what to say. He was maybe 23 years old, trying to make everyone happy, and here was Steve Largent, model citizen and team leader, lecturing him on the importance of telling the truth. Jeff felt terrible. He didn't sleep that night.

When Jeff ultimately summoned the courage to apologize, Steve was understanding and supportive and just a complete gentleman, as always. As for Jeff Pinneo, he learned a life lesson that served him well; he went on to become president and CEO of Horizon Air.

"We Have an Emergency"

Stories from the road weren't always funny. A bomb scare once forced us to return to the airport, de-plane and wait several hours as canine units did their thing. There were no bombs on the plane, fortunately, but piles of smelly jocks and sweat-soaked T-shirts made those poor dogs earn their chow that day.

Another time, as we rolled down the runway en route back to Seattle, players began screaming about a burning wing. "We have an emergency back here!" a flight attendant told the pilots. The captain jammed on the brakes just as the big bird's nose was rising off the runway. We skidded to an abrupt stop as the end of the runway neared.

Only until after our arrival back at the gate did the pilot tell us there had been no fire. When they pressurized the fuel tank, excess fuel shot out the wingtip, creating the illusion of smoke. But you could've fooled us.

CHAPTER 11

Jim Zorn

W ho would have expected one of the NFL's most exciting quarterbacks, and one of the Seahawks' biggest stars, to be seen tooling around town in an old yellow Volkswagen? That was Jim Zorn.

Here was this happy-go-lucky California kid who looked like he literally just fell out of some fraternity on campus, with the boyish haircut, blue jeans and flannel shirt. No one would have guessed it, but there was a gunslinger hiding inside the choir boy.

"Nobody could throw on the run as well as me," Zorn would say years later. "I really believed that."

In an offense built around his strength, Zorn was an instant hit with coaches, teammates and fans. He was best on the move, amazingly accurate and always a threat to take off downfield. The sixth sense he developed with Steve Largent always seemed to bail out the offense at its moment of greatest need.

"If there was one quarterback I wanted to grab and just lift up and smash," Oakland's Phil Villapiano once said, "it was Jim Zorn. But I couldn't catch the guy."

Fun to Watch

The nine-win seasons of 1978 and 1979 were a credit to Jim Zorn and the unpredictable offense he led. Jim was only the third player to top 10,000 yards passing in his first four years. He would pass for 20,122 yards and 107 touchdowns, but numbers could never define Jim Zorn.

The feel for the rush, the ability to improvise, the sense that anything could happen on any given play.

"I would hope when fans remember our play in the early years that it was the most exciting football they had ever seen," Jim said. "Because that's the way I remember it."

First Things First

Jim Zorn's first Kingdome memory might also be his favorite. The St. Louis Cardinals were in town for that 1976 opener.

"I saw Steve Largent come open on an out-and-up, but I overthrew him. He dove for it and flew through the air, completely horizontal, and made this incredible catch. I

knew he was special right then. And that kind of play typified us in those first few years. We were scratching and claw-
ing and scrambling around, making plays and having fun."

Hitting the Bottle Hard

Jim Zorn and Steve Largent were roommates at training
camp. In about 1980, when Jacob Green was just starting out, he witnessed one of the few times when Z-man
actually lost his temper. In fact, it might have been the
only time, at least in front of us. And this is classic Zorn.

While some guys were undoubtedly chasing coeds or
otherwise wreaking havoc in whatever little spare time we
had, Jim Zorn was building one of those miniature ships
inside a bottle. Remember those? This one was all but finished when Jacob paid a visit to Jim and Steve.

Of course, Largent was already a big star in the
league and Jimmy was one of the most recognized
young quarterbacks around. They were chatting when
Steve picked up this bottle and dropped it by accident.
The bottle didn't break, but the ship was in pieces.

Steve said something along the lines of "oops"—
maybe the only time Steve Largent ever said "oops" for
dropping anything. And it was from his quarterback, but it
wasn't a pass. Jacob was watching this thinking, hey, that's
too bad, but Jim can probably fix it. But Jim suddenly
lost it. He grabbed the bottle and just smashed it, then
stormed out of the room and jumped on his bike. Jacob
was watching this as a rookie, and he learned something
about the NFL.

"This is the real thing. These guys are competitive
even when it's just a ship in a bottle."

Steve and Jacob laughed about that later on, but Jim was serious.

Beating the Raiders

It was Ken Stabler who tossed four interceptions during a 1978 game in the Kingdome. Jim Zorn won that duel as the Hawks beat Oakland for the first time. Seattle would win the next three in the series.

The Raiders won the next five after that, and when the Seahawks finally broke through with a win in 1983, Zorn actually lost his job. Seattle got only 13 yards passing from Jimmy that day. Eight turnovers and a 75-yard punt return by Paul Johns helped the Seahawks prevail, 38-36. By the end of that season, Jim was on the bench and the Seahawks were in the play-offs for the first time. It was a bittersweet time for Jim and the beginning of the end for his career in Seattle.

"I had worked so long to get to that point, so I was excited. But it was also a tough day for me because I wanted to play."

Jim Zorn Meets Larry Bird

Jim Zorn was the big name in town during our early years, so it made sense when KIRO-TV hired him to fill in for Wayne Cody on sports. They threw him on the sports desk and Jim would read the sports news. Like everyone else, Jim found out broadcasting isn't as easy as it looks.

Jim's daughter, Sarah, had just been born, so Jim was accustomed to reading bedtime stories. Problem was, that's how he read the news. And once he got going, there was sometimes no stopping him. He'd just keep reading the TelePrompTer.

One time, Jim kept reading even after receiving the "S.O.T." cue that informed broadcasters to let the audio from "sound on tape" take over. Jim just kept talking right over an interview with Larry Bird. And the producer was putting his finger over his lips, trying to tell Jim to shut up. But Jim kept reading, this time in a low voice, so you could hear Jim whispering during a Larry Bird interview.

That might have been when Jim decided he'd go into coaching instead of broadcasting.

On Top of His Game

Offensive coordinator Jerry Rhome couldn't believe the Broncos were still playing man coverage. Were they crazy? Jerry couldn't get Jim Zorn on the phone fast enough. The call was a basic out-and-up that Steve Largent turned into a spin cycle for Louis Wright, the Denver corner. Steve turned Louis all the way around and was just wide open. Jimmy scrambled to his right, pump faked and found his target almost without effort. Seattle won that 1979 game at the Kingdome, the Seahawks' sixth win in eight games.

"It just seemed so much like what our offense was capable of doing when we were playing well," Jim said of that play. "On a critical play that you had to have, it just seemed so easy."

There was a great confidence on that team offensively and it started with Jerry Rhome, who felt like we'd just keep attacking no matter what the defense could do. Steve averaged almost 19 yards a catch that year.

Losing His Touch

How quickly things can change. By 1980, Jim Zorn was feeling a bit lost and the offense wasn't so dangerous. One play typified Jimmy's growing frustrations. With David Hughes running uncovered down the middle of the field, Jim stepped up to make what he considered a pretty routine throw. But the ball sailed long, and Jerry Rhome was waiting on the phone from the pressbox when Jim got back to the sideline.

"There's a real fine line between being a success and being an also-ran in this game. If you want to be a great quarterback, you have to complete that pass down the middle of the field. You just have to complete it."

Those were two plays that Jim has always remembered, the one to Largent in 1979 that seemed so easy, and the one that missed David Hughes in the clear. A real fine line, indeed.

End of the Road

Jim was finished as the starter by mid-1983 and gone after the next season. The kid from Cal Poly-Pomona had started 100 games in nine memorable seasons with the Hawks.

"At times it was an absolute blur. Life changing ... so many lasting friendships ... I met my wife ... I felt embraced by the community just as we embraced the community in those early years. That comes with being a new franchise and everyone's excited to have you here. We established a tradition on this new team as being exciting and fun to watch and all that."

CHAPTER 12

Pete, Wayne and the Gang

One of the first contracts the team ever negotiated wasn't with a player. It was with KIRO radio to broadcast the games.

The station's four-man team of Pete Gross, Wayne Cody, Don Heinrich and engineer Norm Graham was about to shrink by one. Heinrich, the University of Washington legend and former New York Giants star, was leaving to take a similar job with the 49ers.

By then it was readily apparent, even to me, that it was time to start looking for my "life's work," as Jack Patera always put it. Little did I know that it would find me.

Wayne Cody was larger than life.

I had dabbled in broadcasting even as a player, but I hadn't even officially retired from football when Pete called my wife, Sharon, with an opportunity. While I was over in Spokane for a charity golf tournament, Pete relayed to Sharon what in my heart I already knew.

"Steve is never going to be a Largent. He may be able to squeeze out another year or two, but we have an opportunity for him at KIRO."

There were three jobs open: doing the color on radio, doing a magazine-format show five nights a week on TV and filling in for Wayne on TV sports. Pete gave Sharon the tough sell.

"Steve will never have an opportunity like this again. To come in cold like this in the 10th or 11th market in the country and go right to work, that just doesn't happen."

And Pete was right. I retired on a Friday and within three weeks, I was already working at KIRO. For a decade it was the time of my life, the greatest and sometimes craziest learning experience a guy could ever hope to have.

The Incomparable Pete Gross

In the face of all that seemed to be realistic and apparent, Pete Gross was that positive voice. When you listened to Pete call games on the radio, you felt it was going to be better next week or even the next series or the next play. There was always that chance that it could be Zorn-to-Largent for a touchdown, or Curt Warner going around the right side for six, or Dave Brown intercepting a pass and returning it for a touchdown.

There was always that possibility when you listened to Pete broadcast a game. That's one of the reasons everybody took a liking to him. He was remarkably upbeat, always positive about the people whom he covered, the teams that he covered. He genuinely liked those people and they genuinely liked him.

I'm sure Pete's wife, Bev, has heard enough stories that he should be beatified or something. And I'm certain that Pete was in some way, shape or form actually human, and I'm sure his daughters would say the same thing. But what a guy.

Coach Patera angered a lot of people, especially in the press, but that never seemed to affect Pete. He didn't take it personally at all. I think he genuinely liked Jack and thought that Jack was actually doing a good job, even though sometimes a lot of people didn't see it. And I think Jack genuinely respected Pete, not because he was necessarily a homer or anything like that, but just that Pete was almost nauseatingly positive all the time.

And the people Pete covered could trust him. We knew he wouldn't turn what we said around on us. We could level with him and he would keep things in confidence. He was just that kind of guy. It's fun to listen to some of the old tapes and to listen to him with the calls of the game. Because the energy and enthusiasm was just wonderful. It got you excited all over again for some of those big plays, Steve Largent making a catch and Dave Krieg with a big pass.

Football is a very visceral game. It's a game of sights and sounds. If you're a player, it's a game of smells. The smell of the cut grass on the field, the smell of the locker room, those kinds of things. And to hear Pete calling a game, it just conjures up all those great memories. And certainly for a lot of fans, too, it reminds them of those days when there was a lot to cheer about. We're getting back to that again and that's fun. It's too bad Pete isn't around to see it.

Cast of Characters

Norm Graham was a story unto himself. He was a Christian Scientist who never married and a guy who preferred reading Bible verses in his hotel room to joining Pete, Wayne and me for dinner.

He was a wonderful engineer and very knowledgeable. He'd get a per diem to travel, and he'd always return about two-thirds of it after the trip, because he'd just down a few burgers at White Castle.

Norm was just a wonderful guy and so completely opposite from Wayne in so many ways. Norm almost never went out with us, and Wayne would go from dinner to the racetrack even if it meant driving 150 miles.

Here I'm the kid, I'm learning the business and I'm still kind of identifying more with players than I am with being a broadcaster and yet I'm traveling with this three-ring circus.

The chemistry of that group was simply terrific.

Down for the Count

Perhaps only the first win in Seahawks history could upstage Wayne's impromptu pregame performance back in October 1976.

The affair was in Tampa and Wayne had worked a college game in Seattle the day before, so he was a wreck after flying all night to Florida. He hadn't slept, and the steamy conditions took a heavy toll. Wayne weighed 325 for all anyone knew.

And by then he had eaten everything on the plane and probably stopped at a couple of Whataburgers on the drive to the stadium.

We were out there for pregame warmups and Wayne was sitting on the end of the bench down on the field, just trying to get some rest. And he started to doze off. His head bobbed a little bit. He woke up. The eyes closed again and his head dropped a little further and his chin hit his chest. He woke up again.

Then finally he dozed off and before long he started leaning to his right. And he fell right off the end of the bench just like a Benny Hill pratfall—boom! He fell right on his side like a sack of hammers and knocked the wind out of himself.

With Wayne, he had a tough time getting off the ground, so he's flopping like a turtle. He couldn't breathe.

At that point one of our defensive linemen, Bob Lurtsema, walked over and told Wayne to cut out the drinking the night before games. Called him a sloppy drunk and the whole thing.

Bob walked away and Wayne had no chance to even respond because he was still out of breath.

Wayne eventually dragged himself back onto the bench and worked the game. And the thing was, Wayne never drank, and it's a good thing he didn't that day. The game lasted forever thanks to 35 penalties between the teams, by far the most in a game involving Seattle.

For Wayne, that must have been torture.

Better Make That Order To Go

Wayne always did the pregame show, but once the game started, he was free until postgame interviews.

Sometimes he'd go sit out in the stands or the press box, and have a corn dog or a ton of popcorn.

So, we're down in San Diego, the game starts and we don't see Wayne. And then, sure enough, after the game, there's Wayne down in the locker room where he's supposed to be.

When it was time to drive over to the airport, I was the one responsible for getting the car and opening it up. So I grab the keys, open the car up, and the smell inside the car was overwhelming. Garlic and shrimp.

At the start of the game, Wayne, who was going to interview players at the end of the football game about the performance on the field that day, left to go to see the dogs run for a while, and then after making a few bets on the dogs, he swung by Anthony's Star of the Sea.

The guy had bought two huge to-go orders of the shrimp scampi in garlic sauce, plus a bag of pumpernickel crisps. And then for the better part of the fourth quarter, he sat out in the parking lot at Jack Murphy Stadium and ate these huge garlic shrimp. He would open the door and throw the skins under the car.

And so the inside of the car was permeated with garlic and shrimp and pumpernickel crisps, and when I moved the car, it looked like an entire school of fish had exploded under our vehicle. Just awash in shrimp skins. And God knows, I mean, there were sea gulls suddenly just coming in from Monterrey and all over Northern California because of the meal that was out in the parking lot.

And of course Wayne had one extra order that he kept with him for the plane. Once he opened that on the plane, the smell made the players think they had a great meal coming. But, alas, they were stuck with the same dry cheeseburgers they always had, and Wayne scarfed down more shrimp scampi with pumpernickel crisps on the plane.

He was all grease from the ends of his fingers to his elbows.

There were some things on a road trip that were just more important. And the incredible thing about Wayne was that you never would have known that he hadn't watched every play of the game.

He knew exactly what he was doing and he always did just a great job, and it was always so entertaining. Right down to the last pumpernickel crisp.

Pete Gross, Ticket Broker

So we go down to Los Angeles for the AFC title game after the '83 season and it was, as usual, Pete Gross and Wayne Cody and me driving to the game in the Lincoln Town Car that Wayne always rented.

We pull into the media parking lot and all these folks dressed in black and silver are standing around, waiting to get into the stadium. In those days, and happily so, we didn't wear any team-issued clothing revealing our identities as members of the Seahawks' broadcast crew. The Coliseum was no place to be seen wearing enemy garb. We just looked like three nimrods walking into the stadium with our little bags, which was bad enough in itself.

So we get to the press gate and because traffic was so bad that day, we were running late. Pete desperately needed to find will-call so he could leave four tickets he promised to a friend, but time was running short and none of us knew where to find the ticket window.

Fortunately, as we're going through the turnstiles there's a guy with all the official garb, the Raiders stuff, standing right there. He was an official with the Raiders, he told us, and would be happy to deliver Pete's tickets to will call. Pete thanked the guy and we headed up to the press box. Problem solved.

Well, we're minutes away from kickoff and here comes Gary Wright, the Seahawks' PR director at the time, into the press box with the bad news. Pete's increasingly frantic friend was downstairs wondering why his good buddy failed to leave the tickets at will-call.

Turns out our friendly Raiders official was just some schmo and now he and three of his pals were sitting somewhere in Pete Gross's very good seats, and there was nothing any of us could do. Poor Pete had to go forward and do the game with his friend standing outside wondering why his great buddy Pete failed to come through.

Under Water with Wayne

One of the worst games we played was October 9, 1977, at New England. The Patriots beat us, 31-0, and it rained like an old man was building a boat for all the animals out in the back yard.

There was a big crown on the field in Foxboro and the water was coming off in waves. It was lapping over our feet on the sidelines. They were lowering the plow on the snow-removal truck and using it like a giant Squeegee on the field.

And poor Wayne Cody was reporting from the sidelines. He would click the on-off switch on his microphone and invariably he'd be standing in a puddle of water and get himself shocked.

So he's trying to report. "Yeah, PETE, I saw this INCRED-ible play, what a great BLOCK down here." Meantime, he's just soaked, right down to the skin stretched across that 300-and-some-odd-pound frame.

And so at halftime, we all come in. Now, remember, this is the old days in the NFL. People didn't bring two and three changes of jerseys and shoes. You came in soaking wet and you went back out soaking wet.

But Wayne had thrown his carry-on bag in a corner of the locker room. So we look over and he's changing his clothes. Well, we go back out there and it rains harder. If it's possible, he's even wetter than he was in the first half.

Meantime, during the game, the windows in the press box were fogging up so bad that Norm Graham, the broadcast engineer, had to pull his boxers from his overnight bag and wipe the window so Pete could see what was happening out on the field. Over in the coaches' booth, our offensive coordinator, Jerry Rhome, finally threw a chair to break the glass so he could see the field. All this to say we lost 31 to nothing.

Well, after the game, there's Wayne standing over by his carry-on bag with his trousers stretched across multiple lockers, and he's got a hair dryer. Let's face it, this is like trying to stand on the deck of a sailing ship and blow into the sail and get it to move.

So we all go out to the airport and he gets in this Alaska Airlines 727 and he's just jammed against the window with Pete in the middle and Norm Graham on the aisle. And Norm was a pretty big guy.

We had to stop at least once to refuel. By the time we landed in Seattle and got off the plane, Wayne's entire backside was imprinted into the foam core of the seat. Not only was the fabric on the outside of the seat wet, the metal frame through the foam was wet.

When you have 300 pounds of pressure pushing on water through a fabric, it's eventually going to find its way through. He'd have created diamonds had he any sort of carbon products in his pockets.

Well, Wayne just swore that they had to replace the entire seat. There was no chance anybody could ever sit there again because he had just absolutely destroyed it. Just the sight of him drying his trousers and then what he did to that poor seat was just awful.

Little Man, Big Voice

Pete was this little guy with a voice that reached frequencies known only to the canine ear. Dogs would come running when he'd scream, "Touchdown, Seahawks!" into that microphone.

And it was just such a dichotomy in the setting with all these big, hulking football players and this big coach, Jack Patera, and then there was Pete.

A Night to Remember

The night Pete was inducted into the Ring of Honor was just unbelievable. He was so incredibly brave. The cancer was killing him and, unbeknownst to us at the time, he would die within 48 hours of that Monday night victory over Denver on November 30, 1992.

Pete barely had enough strength to walk out to that microphone, but to talk and to give the fans one more "Touchdown, Seahawks!" … I think he summoned every bit of strength for that whole day just for that night, just so he could come down to the stadium and do that.

Wayne Cody and I were up in the 300 level hanging over the edge and we were the ones who pulled back the canvas cover to reveal Pete's name. We were a mile high in

Pete Gross waves goodbye to the Kingdome faithful on November 30, 1992.

the air but we were both just crying like babies, the two of us. It was tough, real tough.

I remember Tom Flores getting teary-eyed in his press conference after the game, saying the game ball was going to go to Pete. And then I got a call on Wednesday of that week from Pete's son-in-law.

"Pete's going fast. You might want to come by the house."

And so I did. My wife Sharon stayed downstairs with Pete's wife, Bev, and they talked for a while. One of Pete's daughters had yet to arrive, but her plane was due any time. The other two girls were there and the one son-in-law was there. He took me upstairs. Peter was lying in his bed and he was just so frail. There was just nothing left to him, hardly, and he was that jaundiced color, that yellow, and his eyes were that color and he barely could open his eyes and look up.

And so I just talked with him for a few minutes. He didn't say much. He kind of smiled one time and then that was that. I kissed him on the forehead and left. And I got a call later that night that he had died.

I was the sports anchor for KIRO-TV at the time and I couldn't even get through the lead-in of his obituary. Gary Justice, the news anchor at the time, sent me home, so I didn't even do sports that night.

We found out later that all of Pete's daughters were at his side when he passed. It was almost as though he was waiting until all the family got there. And they had just gotten there. It was pretty remarkable.

The team went 2-14 that year. Knowing Peter, he would make the joke that if he hadn't died of cancer, that '92 season would have killed him. That's one thing about Peter, too. He had this really funny, almost sinister sense of humor. I swear he'd make that joke.

End of the Road

Wayne lost his best friend when Pete passed away. Different as they were, Pete and Wayne had worked together at KIRO for close to 20 years. They were like brothers. Pete would be doing his sportscast on live radio when, out of nowhere, Wayne would put a match to Pete's script. Pete, the pro that he was, wouldn't miss a beat. And once Pete was gone, things weren't the same.

Wayne's health declined steadily, but he lived a great life for 60-some years. Having talked to him often in those last months, Wayne wasn't the happiest guy in the world, but he wasn't totally unhappy either. He knew he'd done a lot in those years.

He had a quote and I used it in the videotape I made for his memorial service.

"I never ask God to give me anything," Wayne would say, "I just ask him not to take anything away."

That was always pretty telling, because what Wayne had was his work and his friends and his fun. And when they took away his work, that hurt him badly.

It was tough on him because he was for so long the toast of the town. Literally, the biggest name in town. And it hurt him, but he always had great friends, right to the end.

I took lunch over to his condo in Kent a number of times and we'd sit around and talk. I called him in the hospital when he went in several times. And then the last time, he just never came out.

Pete and Wayne. I miss those guys to this day.

FIRST IMPRESSION: Wayne Cody

It was almost without fail that everybody who ever met Wayne Cody in my business, generally as an athlete, heard him first on the radio. He interviewed you. So you didn't know what he looked like. You hadn't seen him before you heard him.

Back in 1976, he was in Seattle doing his *Sportsline* radio show and the team would line up people to come sit on the telephone and talk to Wayne after dinner.

And that was my first ever contact with Wayne Cody. Here is this incredible voice, the great sports-type voice that's on the line asking me questions. He's jovial and funny. And it's just great fun. You're a young rookie in Cheney, Washington, wherever the hell that is, doing this interview on the phone.

But at some point, probably before one of the games we played back in Seattle, he came out to practice one day. And he walks up and introduces himself.

"I'm Wayne Cody."

Holy cow, I thought. Yes, I guess you are. I know by the voice, but it just sort of didn't add up. He's five foot ten, maybe, and pushing three big ones... maybe more. He could have been on the other side of 300 looking back. That's the first impression.

Easy Come, Easy Go

Corky Trewin, longtime team photographer, was in his mid-20s when Wayne took him along to the dog track one Friday night on the road in 1979. Corky didn't have much money and he wasn't much of a gambler. Wayne, on the other hand, would route his travel plans through Vegas if at all possible. Out of the blue, the Seahawks' bigger-than-life radio sideline reporter whipped out $100 and essentially ordered Corky to play the dogs.

Corky obliged and as luck would have it, he walked away with $800.

The next night, Wayne and Corky were among a group of nine that went out to a fancy dinner. Out of the blue, again, Wayne announced that Corky would be picking up the tab, end of discussion. Just like that, the entire $800 was gone, having vanished as quickly as it appeared.

"When good fortune comes your way, spend it another way," Wayne always theorized. What a gem.

CHAPTER 13

Silver Linings

The 1992 Seahawks produced the worst offense in NFL history, a forgettable 2-14 record and, incredibly, the NFL's defensive player of the year in Cortez Kennedy. Looking back, the way that team stuck together despite such obvious fault lines made that season more rewarding than anyone would have a right to believe.

Coach Tom Flores and defensive coordinator Tom Catlin held things together remarkably well. This was a team that never scored more than 17 points in a game, and yet opponents topped 21 points only five times. Offensive coordinator Larry Kennan, who won a Super Bowl with Flores and the Raiders nearly a decade before, marveled at the unity.

Tom Flores did a wonderful job holding the 1992 team together.

"Normally when the defense is really good and the offense sucks, you get some bitching and moaning. Well, none of that happened because of Tom Catlin and his great respect for Tom Flores and the way he handled all of us.

"It was a wonderful job of pulling that team together. I remember several of the veteran players telling the younger guys in offensive meetings, 'Look, guys, you don't realize what a good guy you're working for until you go several other places in this league and find out. Tom Flores is a really class man. We need to win for him.' It was really very touching."

Paul Moyer didn't coach all that long, but he actually called that 1992 season his most fun as an assistant. They were so close on defense and there was really no pressure once the season started going south.

Sweet Victory

The '92 Hawks staggered into their Monday night meeting with Denver at 1-10. This was the night Pete Gross courageously went into the Ring of Honor, and in one of the least artistic games ever endured, the Seahawks somehow managed to reward Pete with a 16-13 overtime victory.

With an injured John Elway watching, presumably in horror, the teams combined for 20 penalties, 25 first downs and eight third-down conversions in 37 tries.

Seattle's Stan Gelbaugh was a great guy and a less-than-great NFL quarterback, but he was actually pretty effective running a two-minute offense. With no timeouts and 62 seconds left in regulation, Stan led the offense 70 yards to the tying touchdown as time expired.

Kicker John Kasay missed a 33-yard try midway through overtime, only to atone with the game-winning 32-yarder a few minutes later.

1.5 Yards Per Play

The worst offense in league history played at peak efficiency on December 13, 1992, at Veterans Stadium. Unfortunately, Buddy Ryan's vaunted Eagles defense was across the line of scrimmage that day. The Eagles barely won in overtime, 20-17, despite controlling the ball for more than 47 minutes. Philly ran 95 offensive plays that day, none of them particularly memorable.

The Seahawks managed only 87 net yards and an almost comically meager 1.5 yards per play.

"Honest to God, we played as well as we could play," Larry Kennan said. "We played our asses off. We could have been minus yards. They were awesome."

None Better Than Tez

Chuck Knox was giddy when the Seahawks landed Cortez Kennedy in the first round of the 1990 draft. The rest of the league found out why in that 1992 season. Inspired by the death of close friend and former college teammate Jerome Brown, Cortez became unblockable.

Tez finished that '92 season with 14 sacks and 92 tackles, including 76 solo stops. Twenty-eight of his tackles came behind the line of scrimmage, a team record. Those are ridiculous numbers for a defensive tackle or anyone else.

Teams tried to triple-team him, and still Tez got free. Quickness set him apart. The pressure he put on offenses allowed Seattle's defense to gamble and force turnovers.

Tez seemed amused in 1993 when the rival Broncos introduced newly signed guard Brian Habib as the player they needed to block the NFL's reigning defensive player of the year.

"Who is this Brian Habib?" Tez asked innocently.

Habib was a super-sized lineman who played his college ball at the University of Washington. Brian was big and strong, but not particularly mobile. And, like so many of his contemporaries, he was no match for Cortez Kennedy.

Brian rarely got a hand on Tez during his five years with the Broncos. The trend continued in practice after the Hawks signed Habib as a free agent in 1998. This was no knock on Brian, who played a dozen years and won a Super Bowl with Denver. Tez was simply the best.

CHAPTER 14

The Jake

For all that's made of how the Raiders won with the wild-eyed Matuszaks of the NFL underworld, I don't think enough is made of how the Seahawks conducted business. Character was a major factor in acquiring talent, especially in the early years, and Jacob Green was one of the all-time good guys. He still is.

So when I asked Jake to recount his greatest memories from a career that spanned 178 games and 116 quarterback sacks, it was fitting that three of his all-timers had nothing to do with him.

The first was Curt Warner's professional debut and that 60-yard run on his first NFL carry. "That's when I knew we had a guy who could take us there," Jacob said.

Kenny Easley's three-interception game at San Diego in 1984 furnished Jacob with another memory he still cherishes. Safeties weren't supposed to dominate games like that. Seattle hammered the Chargers 24-0 at Jack Murphy Stadium. "It was one of the finest games I ever saw any Seahawk player have. Kenny was just absolutely in control of the game."

Steve Largent's 40-yard catch in that '83 playoff game also ranked near the top on Jacob's list. "Everybody knew it was going to be a corner route and they still couldn't cover it."

Jake singled out those three moments even though he wasn't on the field for any of them. He always was such a team guy.

Emotions Ran High

Jacob led the team with nine tackles and 2.5 sacks that December day in 1984. The Hawks outlasted the Raiders in a wild-card playoff game at the Kingdome, but that was only part of the story. Jacob played that game without practicing the week before. He'd been down in Houston with his beloved father, who was dying from cancer, and when he returned to Seattle after a couple days, Jacob wouldn't stay long.

Jaycee Green died that week at age 65. Jacob went back for the funeral, then turned around and came back to Seattle in time for the game. And what a game it was. It might have been the best game Jacob ever played. He always played with emotion, but this was obviously different. "As a team, we physically dominated the Raiders that day."

Jacob Green bears down on Dan Fouts.

As an individual, and in every way, Jacob dominated his matchup with Henry Lawrence, the Raiders' big right tackle. Jacob later said he thought he cried on every play, just thinking of his father. And after the game, he remembered feeling more drained, both emotionally and physically, than he ever felt before.

Jacob Green had won a football game, knocking off the defending Super Bowl champs, but he had lost his father. He gets choked up thinking about it decades later.

Three of a Kind

Easley, Warner and Largent were the finest players Jacob Green ever played with. That much isn't in doubt with Jacob.

"But when it comes to going into a dark alley anywhere, anytime, I knew that Joe Nash and Jeff Bryant had my back."

Those three started together in a 3-4 defense for eight consecutive seasons ending with Cortez Kennedy's emergence in 1991. Jacob said they knew offensive lines couldn't handle them man to man.

"We were all just competitors. People talked about guys like Joe Nash as being an overachiever. Joe was not an overachiever. Joe Nash was as tough a football player as I ever met, as big a competitor, as strong as anybody."

Jeff "Boogie" Bryant was a mellow, quiet guy, but just as mean and nasty and tough as could be on the field. Anthony Munoz hated to play against him, and Anthony is in the Hall of Fame. Boogie would beat him to the outside and hit him up under the chin. Jacob said it always drove Munoz crazy.

But Jacob was the best of the bunch, just a great athlete with a knack for the big play. The quickness, the ability to get upfield and get around guys ... Jacob had it all. When the ball fell on the ground in front of Jake, he was one of those guys who would pick it up and make something happen. He could run away from people.

And when you turned up the noise in the Kingdome, Jacob couldn't be stopped. Remember some of those games with the Raiders? Marc Wilson couldn't even get the play called. It was comical.

The Ultimate Warriors

Teams don't bring as many players to training camp these days, so it's tough to practice as hard as guys did back when Jacob Green was playing. Some of those practices were beyond tough. They were brutal.

Injuries took a heavy toll on the defensive line one year, leaving Joe Nash, Jeff Bryant and Jake as the only guys available for the afternoon practice. Jacob and Joe had been to the Pro Bowl by this time, so they were established players, guys who didn't have to take all the reps in two-a-days.

But on this day, there was no one else. Jacob, Jeff and Joe took every snap in every drill that afternoon: seven on seven, run thud, blitz drill, everything. There was a point just before the team period when Chuck Knox came over to the huddle offering some relief. "You three have been going every play today. I'm thinking about calling off practice early, or at the very least getting some guys to put up front here to let you guys take off your equipment and go take a knee."

That kind of offer comes along once in a career, if that. But Jeff Bryant, who rarely said much of anything, looked at the other two guys and waved off the head man. "Coach, by the time we took off all our pads ... we might just as well go on and finish practice."

So they did. They finished every play of the practice. There was a point in there where they put Fredd Young in as a down lineman to get a few rushes at the quarterback, but otherwise it was just those three, all day, every play, no questions asked.

They were beat when that day finally ended, but that was the attitude that made those guys so tough.

And Chuck appreciated it. His d-line coach, George Dyer, told those three to go have a beer, take the night off, do whatever they wanted. That kind of recognition, from a coach or a peer, means 100 times more to players than the accolades they get from anyone else.

Jake and Pete

Jacob Green's annual golf tournament has raised more than $1 million for the Fred Hutchinson Cancer Research Center in Seattle. The cause is so dear to Jacob, in particular, after what happened to his own father and, nearly a decade later, to the other father figure in his life.

Pete Gross was so much more than our radio play-by-play man. Everybody loved him, but Jacob's relationship with Pete had grown into an enduring friendship. Ask Jacob about his dad or about Pete and the tears will flow, without fail. As big and strong and tough as Jake is, he's so gentle and caring.

Pete's wife, Bev, has often talked about how much Pete thought of Jacob as a man, as a player, as a husband—all those things. Pete just really thought Jacob was a terrific person, and he was right.

CHAPTER 15

As I Was Saying...

When the original "Tales" book went to press in 2004, the Seahawks had three postseason victories to show for their first 28 seasons. They've added 13 in the intervening 12 seasons, one of the biggest being the 34-14 domination of Carolina with a berth in Super Bowl XL on the line. It was the signature victory in what stands as the Seahawks' signature season.

The memory of team owner Paul Allen raising the 12th Man flag before that epic victory stands apart from all the others. Something about that moment said we've finally arrived. And we did it in one of the great stadiums in the NFL, with an owner who literally rescued pro football in the Pacific Northwest.

The current and most successful chapter in Seahawks history began when Paul Allen purchased the team in 1997. He hired one of the NFL's finest coaches, Mike Holmgren, and pushed to build one of the NFL's finest stadiums, Qwest Field (since renamed CenturyLink Field). It all came together during that 2005 season.

Paul, a driving force with Bill Gates in the formation of Microsoft before Gates became the face of the computing industry, had preferred to stay in the background as an NFL owner. Now he was standing atop the south end zone at Qwest while the NFL's loudest fans—fans responsible for inciting more opponent false-start penalties than any others—saluted him. For the fans to see Paul recognized for what he had done, it was just a marvelous moment. The cheering went on and on. It still reverberates.

For a while, though, few could have seen it coming. That 2005 season opened with the Seahawks in a bit of a transition. They had lost three times to the Rams in the previous season, including at home in the wild-card round of the playoffs. Backup quarterback Trent Dilfer, a stabilizing force behind the scenes, had requested and won a trade that offseason. His departure to Cleveland represented a loss underrated at the time. Dilfer had become such a valuable go-between for starter Matthew Hasselbeck and the coaching staff. He was a calming influence on the sideline as well.

It would take a while for Hasselbeck and Holmgren to find their comfort zone during that 2005 season.

When they did, man, it was a beautiful thing to watch. Matthew had a career year: 24 touchdowns, only nine interceptions and a career-best passer rating of 98.2. That 24-touchdown figure easily could have been 40 if the Seahawks hadn't been such a strong running team that season. More on that in a bit.

Holmgren always believed in running his West Coast offense through his quarterback. He'd done it with Joe Montana and Steve Young and Brett Favre before, winning championships with each of them. In Seattle, Holmgren also had an MVP running back in Shaun Alexander and the best offensive line in football. That's what made that 2005 team so complete. The offensive line had been together for years, Hasselbeck was reaching his peak and the defense, featuring a young Lofa Tatupu, was a lot better than people realized.

Even then, it wasn't always easy. There was a tough opening-day loss in the heat at Jacksonville. The pass protection was shaky, to say the least, and Matthew took a beating.

Holmgren came under fire a few weeks later for a play call that left Seattle with a longer try for the tying fourth-quarter field goal at Washington. When the usually reliable Josh Brown bounced one off the upright, the not-yet-best team in Seahawks history was on its way to an overtime defeat and a 2-2 record to start the season.

But there were positive signs even during that disappointing start.

The heart that Bobby Engram showed in the game against Washington stands out. Engram, one of the finest slot receivers of his era, suffered two cracked ribs on the game's first play when Ryan Clark, the Redskins' safety, made Engram pay for pursuing a high ball. Engram stayed in the game and wound up with nine receptions for 106 yards, both game-high totals. But the injury would linger, as rib injuries do.

With a knee injury limiting fellow receiver Darrell Jackson, the Seahawks would turn to the hard-nosed and physical Joe Jurevicius. All he did was score 10 touchdowns that year. There would have been no Super Bowl without him.

Holmgren, being the offensive perfectionist that he was, never could tolerate turnovers from his quarterback. So, when the Jaguars picked off a desperation pass Hasselbeck threw across the field in Week 1, the coach wasn't too happy. He summoned Matthew into his office for the first of two soul-searching sessions that season.

"Look, you're really good," Holmgren told his quarterback. "You can be as good as you want to be. The team really counts on you. That play reminded me of five years ago. You might not complete every ball but that kind of play, that's the play we've got to eliminate."

Hasselbeck understood, but he would be back in the principal's office later in the season, this time after a sideline confrontation at San Francisco. These were two highly competitive men at the peak of their powers. They could be headstrong, but in the end, they always put the team first.

"He and I had a moment there [on the sideline] where he did something and I jumped at him and he kind of jumped at me and then I grabbed him," Holmgren said. "On Monday I called him in and we talked about it. As I look back on it, I think that set the table for just a great finish."

Seattle topped 40 points in two of its next three games. The team won its next five to reach 13-2 before resting starters in the final game with an eye toward the playoffs, where the Redskins would await, quite fittingly. By then, Seattle had won the NFC West by a stunning seven-game margin.

They couldn't have done it without the first league MVP in franchise history. A 50-member media panel gave Shaun Alexander 19 first-place votes. Peyton Manning (13) and Tom Brady (10) trailed well behind. In a lot of ways, Alexander put the Seahawks on the map that season. He was the Seahawks' first true offensive superstar since Steve Largent, the team's only true Hall of Famer until Cortez Kennedy joined him in Canton, retired following the 1989 season.

Alexander set a team record with 1,880 yards, capping five years with at least 1,100 yards and 14 rushing touchdowns per season. His 28 rushing touchdowns in 2005 were a league record at the time. With Pro Bowl fullback Mack Strong and a line featuring Walter Jones, Steve Hutchinson, Robbie Tobeck, Chris Gray and Sean Locklear, Alexander got the tough yards, too. He was perfect on 16 rushes when facing third-and-1. That also led the league.

There were so many other "role" players making contributions the Seahawks absolutely had to have. We mentioned

Jurevicius, whose stiff-arms and overall snarl could inspire. While Holmgren built the nucleus of that team during his run as GM, new president Tim Ruskell filled in the roster with guys like Jurevicius, tight end Ryan Hannam, defensive tackle Craig Terrill, defensive tackle Chuck Darby, Leroy Hill and fellow linebacker Tatupu.

Don't forget about safety Marquand Manuel, either. His unfortunate injury departure from the Super Bowl was an underrated turning point in that bitter loss to Pittsburgh. But let's not dwell on the negative. Fans should remember the feeling of destiny as it built with that unforgettable overtime thriller against the New York Giants. My ears ring just thinking about it. The Giants reached double figures in false starts that day. Their kicker, Jay Feely, missed three times. Josh Brown won it with a 36-yarder in overtime, and Jurevicius overcame a couple uncharacteristic drops to finish with eight catches for 137 yards and two scores. He was one of the newcomers making a difference—making THE difference in a lot of ways.

"It just takes perseverance and character," defensive end Grant Wistrom said afterward. "That's the main thing they did in bringing the guys in here that they brought. They brought guys in here with character. When your back's against the wall, they're going to fight their way out of it."

The Seahawks could feel it. We all could.

"I do believe this is our year," Alexander said.

A Final Thought

On a chilly Saturday evening a few days before Christmas, Ron Callan and I were just hours from broadcasting the Seahawks' game in New York against the Giants. But standing on a street corner in lower Manhattan that night, we thought little of the game. It was December 22, 2001. Three months earlier terrorists flew two jetliners into the World Trade Center. As we neared what had become known as Ground Zero, we noticed the usual harried pace of the city and the excitement of the holidays had vanished, replaced by an almost reverential silence.

There on a wrought-iron fence outside a small church were pictures—hundreds of photographs of those lost in the collapse of the towers. Many had messages of love and remembrance. People stood quietly, some lit candles, some wept. Ron and I introduced ourselves to a nearby cop and explained we were in town for the Giants game the next day. We told him how much the sacrifice his brother officers and firefighters made meant to us and the rest of the country. After a few moments he asked us if we wanted to come inside the barricades and see the site up close ... where 24 hours a day, seven days a week, for months workers had removed the mangled steel and concrete that entombed nearly 3,000 souls.

In those moments we watched recovery crews with a single-minded determination to heal the wound to their city, their country, one small bucketful or shovelful at a time. And we thought, on the one hand, how unimportant a football game seemed at that moment. And on the other, how profoundly lucky we were to be with our friends, to celebrate that fall ritual and return to our loved ones with the promise of future Sundays still to come.

Coach Holmgren, who visited the site earlier in the day, said of the events surrounding September 11, "If someone is telling you they're not affected by it, then I don't think they're being honest. This touches everybody. I mean, everybody."

And that includes those big, tough pro football players who are also sons and brothers and husbands and fathers. They laugh with their pals and they hug their kids and they cry at the loss of loved ones just like the rest of us. And for me, that's the lasting memory from the Seahawks' sideline: boys grown to men and forever bound by Sunday afternoon battles fought with friends for a lifetime.